Refreshingly real and loaded with wisdom, *Becoming MomStrong* has a much-needed message of hope for moms everywhere!

RUTH SCHWENK
Founder of *TheBetterMom.com* and coauthor of *For Better or for Kids*

Heidi's words are a gift to moms everywhere. *Becoming MomStrong* is our invitation to link arms with other moms who understand that raising children who chase after Jesus isn't for the faint of heart. Her simple yet poignant encouragement spurs us on even on those most difficult days.

JEN SCHMIDT
Blogger behind *Balancing Beauty and Bedlam*, host of the Becoming Conference, and *(in)courage* author

In a culture filled with mom shaming, mom guilt, and mommy wars, Heidi St. John's *Becoming MomStrong* breathes grace, encouragement, wisdom, and relief to those mamas looking for a better way than the world's definition of motherhood. This is the book I wish I had read when I first became a mother nearly a decade ago.

ERIN ODOM
Author of *More Than Just Making It: Hope for the Heart of the Financially Frustrated* and creator of *TheHumbledHomemaker.com*

Motherhood isn't for wimps. One minute it can bring you joy and the next it can leave you weak in the knees. I love *Becoming MomStrong* because it points mothers to who they are in Jesus and who He is in them. It offers practical, spiritual guidance for the journey. Moms will be stronger with this book!

KRISTEN WELCH
Bestselling author of *Raising Grateful Kids in an Entitled World*

Heidi's book *Becoming MomStrong* is exactly what we moms need right now. With each passing day it gets easier and easier to just let things slide and let our kids raise themselves. The reality is that we only have "such a time as this" to impart wisdom and truth and good and beautiful things into our kids. This is our time, this is our call, and *Becoming MomStrong* is the rallying cry and strategic message we need.

SARAH MAE
Coauthor of *Desperate: Hope for the Mom Who Needs to Breathe*

This book is more than a book. It's boot camp for a mom's soul. Meet your coach: Heidi St. John. She's also your cheerleader. Heidi will help you discover a strength that you didn't even know you had. With authenticity, urgency, and a great sense of humor, Heidi brings you into her spiritual gym and reveals what it truly means to be MomStrong.

JENNIFER DUKES LEE
Author of *The Happiness Dare* and *Love Idol*

Without apology, Heidi gracefully tackles some of the most strength-zapping dilemmas we (and our loved ones) are facing today—hard things that no previous generation has walked through before.

WENDY SPEAKE
Coauthor of *Triggers: Exchanging Parents' Angry Reactions for Gentle Biblical Responses* and *Life Creative: Inspiration for Today's Renaissance Mom*

We all need someone to come alongside and remind us that we weren't meant to mother in fear, but rather we are to be courageous in the face of the many great challenges that present themselves throughout our parenting journeys. *Becoming MomStrong* is the sounding cry that moms everywhere are looking for. This is a book that extends a hand and reminds us we aren't alone and that together we are strong.

KELLI STUART
Coauthor of *Life Creative: Inspiration for Today's Renaissance Mom* and author of *Like a River from Its Course*

Becoming MomStrong is Heidi's rallying call to moms everywhere to fight for their faith and their families. It's her call to arms, her battle cry for a generation. Heidi shares her story for the benefit of all her readers. Her story is every mom's story—filled with failures, embarrassments, and brokenness. But like her own journey, that's not where ours ends. Our redeeming Savior uses it all for His glory.

RACHAEL CARMAN
Author of *How Many Times Do I Have to Tell You?*; RachaelCarman.com

When I read books on motherhood, I expect to learn and be challenged. But I don't expect to find a riveting page-turner that I can't put down. Heidi had me at the subtitle: *How to Fight with All That's in You for Your Family and Your Faith.* Motherhood is a high-stakes calling, but the journey leads us to places of redemption, restoration, and power in Christ that are life altering and gloriously redemptive. After you read this book, make sure you pass it on. This is a message every Christian mother needs to hear.

ZAN TYLER
Speaker; author; and director of language arts, Bible, and press for Apologia Educational Ministries; *www.apologia.com*

Heidi's biblical perspective on the joys and challenges of motherhood will encourage you and build up your faith. Her down-to-earth way of communicating makes you feel like you are sitting across the table from a friend. Whether you are a soon-to-be-mom, in the middle of raising little ones, or you are supporting a mommy in need, *Becoming MomStrong* is a must read for you!

DEBBIE LINDELL
Lead pastor of James River Church, author, and founder of the Designed for Life Conference

Heidi's engaging writing style and encouraging words dig in and draw a line in the sand of our modern culture. She is a modern-day Joshua, calling on Christian moms to choose to stand and be counted while she simultaneously reminds us to focus on the trustworthiness and strength of the One we serve. *Becoming MomStrong* is a gift to all Kingdom women for such a time as this.

ANGELA O'DELL
Author, speaker, consultant, veteran homeschool mom; *angelaodellblog.com*

Can you imagine having a toddler in your home for twenty-two years in a row? If that doesn't qualify you to write a book entitled *Becoming MomStrong*, I don't know what does. A mother of seven, Heidi St. John gets the weariness and realities of motherhood. But more importantly, she understands parenting in the strength of Almighty God. This book is a call to stop cowering in a corner and to start rising up in faith. This is a much-needed message for this generation of moms.

ARLENE PELLICANE
Speaker and author of several books, including *31 Days to Becoming a Happy Mom*

With refreshing honesty about the struggles we face as mothers, Heidi reminds us that the secret to becoming MomStrong has very little to do with us and *everything* to do with God. She issues the passionate call to not give up, but instead to run in *His* strength as we raise up this next generation!

HEATHER HAUPT
Author of *Raising Knights in Training: Ten Principles for Raising Honorable, Courageous, and Compassionate Boys*

BECOMING MOM STRONG

HOW TO FIGHT

WITH ALL

THAT'S IN YOU

FOR YOUR FAMILY

Heidi St. John

TYNDALE
MOMENTUM™

The nonfiction imprint of
Tyndale House Publishers, Inc.

Visit Tyndale online at www.tyndale.com.

Visit Tyndale Momentum online at www.tyndalemomentum.com.

Visit the author's website at heidistjohn.com.

TYNDALE, Tyndale Momentum, and Tyndale's quill logo are registered trademarks of Tyndale House Publishers, Inc. The Tyndale Momentum logo is a trademark of Tyndale House Publishers, Inc. Tyndale Momentum is the nonfiction imprint of Tyndale House Publishers, Inc., Carol Stream, Illinois.

Becoming MomStrong: How to Fight with All That's in You for Your Family and Your Faith

Copyright © 2017 by Heidi St. John. All rights reserved.

Cover font by NickyLaatz/Creative Market. All right reserved.

Cover gold texture by Studio Denmark/Creative Market. All rights reserved.

Author photograph by Christa Taylor, copyright © 2017. All rights reserved.

Designed by Julie Chen

Published in association with William K. Jensen Literary Agency, 119 Bampton Court, Eugene, Oregon 97404

Unless otherwise indicated, all Scripture quotations are taken from the *Holy Bible,* New Living Translation, copyright © 1996, 2004, 2015 by Tyndale House Foundation. Used by permission of Tyndale House Publishers, Inc., Carol Stream, Illinois 60188. All rights reserved.

Scripture quotations marked NIV are taken from the Holy Bible, *New International Version,*® *NIV.*® Copyright © 1973, 1978, 1984, 2011 by Biblica, Inc.® Used by permission. All rights reserved worldwide.

Scripture quotations marked NCV are taken from the New Century Version.® Copyright © 2005 by Thomas Nelson, Inc. Used by permission. All rights reserved.

Scripture quotations marked ESV are taken from *The Holy Bible,* English Standard Version® (ESV®), copyright © 2001 by Crossway, a publishing ministry of Good News Publishers. Used by permission. All rights reserved.

Scripture quotations marked KJV are taken from the *Holy Bible,* King James Version.

For information about special discounts for bulk purchases, please contact Tyndale House Publishers at csresponse@tyndale.com, or call 1-800-323-9400.

ISBN 978-1-4964-1265-2 (hc)
ISBN 978-1-4964-1266-9 (sc)

Printed in the United States of America

23	22	21	20	19	18	17
7	6	5	4	3	2	1

To my husband,

who leads our family by loving example

and points me to Jesus every day.

And to my children,

who have given me seven beautiful reasons

to be stronger than I ever dared to be.

God has been good to give me

such a precious responsibility.

This book is for Him.

Contents

WELCOME TO THE BATTLE OF YOUR LIFE

*I*t was 5:30 a.m., and my alarm was going off.

"Mama? Mama? Maaaaaammmmaaaaaa! Can you hear me? Are you sleeping?" I opened one eye and tried to focus. It was early, even for my brown-eyed alarm clock. "Sweetheart, why are you awake?" I asked quietly. "Are you okay?"

"Mom," my daughter continued, "the tooth fairy didn't come! I put my tooth right where you said she would find it, but she never came!"

Great. It wasn't even light outside, and I'd had my first failure of the day.

Zero-dark-thirty, and I'd already let someone down.

SUPERNATURAL STRENGTH NEEDED
I wasn't unfamiliar with this feeling—it was a weird mixture of worrying I'd never get it right and simultaneously not caring if

I ever did. I had experienced similar emotions just five hours earlier, when one of my teens—who has all the youthful energy that comes from not being truly responsible for another human being—plopped down next to me on the bed and started talking. Everything was going great . . . until I dozed off in the middle of our conversation. A disheartened "Never mind, Mom" was the last thing I heard that night as I watched my fifteen-year-old shuffle out of the room.

I tried to make excuses for my sudden onset of narcolepsy, explaining that the baby hadn't slept through the night for the past few days, but my words rang hollow to the teenager who had finally decided I was cool enough to engage in late-night conversations—except for the fact that I didn't have any "late night" left in me. *Why can't I be cool at 7:30 instead of 11:30?*

I took a deep breath and looked around the room. I knew there was something—*something*—I needed to remember before I went to bed. After a few minutes, I gave up. My head hit the pillow, where I lay, without sleeping, recounting all the things that were still left on my to-do list from earlier that day. At some point, the list became a lullaby, and I fell asleep.

Now, my six-year-old alarm clock was bringing it all back. That's it—I was supposed to be the tooth fairy last night! I *knew* there was something I was forgetting. On top of my usual roles of wife, lover, mother, cook, chauffeur, teacher, judge, counselor, nurse, birthday party coordinator, and chief laundress, I was also a tooth fairy (part time, of course).

"I'm sorry, sugar," I said to my disappointed child. "Tooth fairies sometimes get lost. Our house is hard to find if you don't have GPS."

My daughter looked confused. "But the tooth fairy doesn't *need* GPS!" she wailed. "She's a *fairy!*"

#momfail

Have you ever seen that hashtag reflected in the eyes of your children? Have you ever looked into the faces of the people who call you Mom and wondered what in the world you got yourself into? Do you ever feel weak and unqualified for the position that is often referred to as "a sacred calling"? Have you ever wished you could transport yourself and your kids back to a simpler time—a time when schools taught math and reading, there was no such thing as the Internet, and churches taught the truth?

I have. I admit that most of the time I feel like I'm in over my head. Maybe you feel that way too. Maybe, like me, you're surrounded by fifteen tons of cold, wrinkled laundry, and you know you need to go to the grocery store, but frankly you just don't care if your tribe eats tonight or not. (Why do they want dinner every. single. night?)

If you're like me, you've been reading the headlines and watching the rapid-fire changes that are taking place in our culture with a fair degree of frustration and fear. Let's face it: moms today are being asked to deal with more than just the basics of motherhood, like packing lunches and making runs to soccer practice; we're grappling with questions that previous generations never even saw coming. Social and spiritual land mines are everywhere. We're constantly assaulted by questions about everything from gender identity to the safety of vaccines. Even the role of government in our parenting decisions is more intrusive than in previous generations.

Today's mothers need a special kind of strength. Yes, we need to be physically strong, but we also need strength of conviction and spiritual fortitude. Today's moms need to be strong in the Lord and in the power of *His* might. We dare not rely on human strength for the current battles we're facing in culture.

I've never met a mom who didn't want to raise strong, healthy kids, but there's a caveat: we can't give our kids what we don't have ourselves. Our children need us to stand up in a culture that is literally shouting, "Stand down!" The schools will tell you that they know better than you do. Don't believe them. The media will tell you that truth is whatever anyone wants it to be and that the role of parents isn't that important. Don't buy it.

Voices from your past might whisper, "You're not ready for this." Don't listen. You can do this! You—the mom in the midst of it all—have been set apart for a job that only you can do: to train your children to hear God's voice and to walk in the truth no matter where our culture is heading.

You might be tempted to shrink back from the challenge or let someone you think is smarter or stronger than you take over. But I want to encourage you—for the sake of your children—to engage in the battle. It's no accident that you're here right now. This is a special generation of mothers who have been called to shepherd a special generation of children.

We have found ourselves in the middle of an epic battle, and if we're going to prevail, we'll need . . .

- to be strong in the Lord,
- to know who we are in Christ, and
- to impart that strength to our kids.

In other words, we need to become *MomStrong*!

YOUR MISSION, SHOULD YOU CHOOSE TO ACCEPT IT— AND YOU MUST!

If you're like me, you might be starting to think you're in over your head when it comes to being the kind of mom God has called you to be . . . and that's okay, because you are. We all are, and that's by design. I believe God knew what He was doing when He decided to give inexperienced young women the responsibility of raising children. In fact, I think God must smile when He sees a mother with her child, teaching and training, loving and correcting, sometimes failing and sometimes getting it right. He understands mothers. After all, He is a Father who has watched His own kids struggle and succeed. He knows firsthand the soul-altering love of a parent. And like mothers, God is always at work to shift and shape, clarify and correct the hearts of His children.

Make no mistake: motherhood is tough, and it's not for the faint of heart. In my twenty-six years of parenting our seven children, I've learned how weak I can be and how strong God is. I've come to believe that God wants to use my role as a mother to give me a glimpse into His Father-heart for all His children. After all, He knows I'm going to need it for the mission I'm on with my own kids.

And yes, whether you're aware of it or not, if you're a mom, you do have a mission—to raise the next generation of teachers, doctors, judges, police officers, grocery store clerks, attorneys, and nurses. Truly, the hand that rocks the cradle rules the world. But wait—there's more. You are also raising the next generation of parents! Look around. It doesn't take long for one generation to hand the baton to the next. And it's up to you, mom, to make sure that when the time comes, your children are strong enough in the Lord to accept the challenge themselves.

What a high calling motherhood is! Our culture may have reduced it to little more than a stopover on the way to something else, but the truth is that motherhood is sacred. You, mom, are shaping the future, one little heart at a time. Everything else pales in comparison.

If you aren't sure where to get the strength you'll need for the journey, keep reading, because this beautifully broken mother of seven would like to give you a gentle hug and a high five as she points you to the true wellspring of life and strength: Jesus.

By the way, it's okay if you're reading this and you don't feel strong. None of us start out strong. The good news is that God doesn't require strength for the journey; He *offers* it. He wants to make us strong, but we have to truly want His strength in order to find it. How do we receive it? By acknowledging our own weakness.

It may feel a little frightening at first, this admission of weakness. But take it from someone who has been there: coming to terms with weakness is liberating. When we finally admit we can't do it on our own and look to Jesus, we're about to be set free. Free from the past. Free from the tyranny of other people's expectations. Free from worry. Free to love. Free to grow. Free to move with confidence into the future. Exchanging our past for a future in Christ and claiming His strength is where becoming MomStrong begins. In Christ, you are more than a conqueror. You are strong, safe, sealed, and secure. You are a channel of the love and life of God for your children.

So where do we start? How can we stand up and be strong

in a culture that marginalizes mothers and puts children at risk by its very definition of family? We go back to the beginning.

God has already given us the blueprint for becoming MomStrong, and that blueprint is found in the Bible. He has entrusted us with bringing up the next generation, and He says that His strength is made perfect in weakness.

So if you're feeling weak today, get ready to find new strength. Get ready to see His heart for you in a new way. It doesn't matter where you are starting. Your inexperience makes you the perfect candidate to receive direction from the One who knows your kids better than you do. Your past doesn't need to define your future. God is in the business of redemption! He makes things new. Strength comes from Him.

By God's grace, we can be strong enough to show the next generation that we serve a mighty God. So join me on the journey, won't you? Let's become MomStrong together!

Heidi St. John
Fall 2017

Chapter 1

GOOD NEWS— YOUR KIDS CAME WITH A MANUAL!

I like manuals. Luckily for me, most things come with one. Your car came with a manual. So did your TV and your Crock-Pot. Last week, I actually bought an eyeliner manual. You know, because, really, I'm just making that up as I go too.

When it comes to parenting, there are a lot of great books out there. But MomStrong moms are looking for more than advice—we're looking for wisdom. And God tells us that the beginning of wisdom is found in knowing the Lord (see Psalm 111:10). The way we find out what God's character is like is by reading His Word. Every other book out there (including this one) pales in comparison to that singular literary masterpiece. It's the only book you need.

I learned this lesson from an older couple when my now-grown kids were still very young. In fact, it's etched in my memory forever.

One Saturday afternoon when my husband, Jay, and I were rookie parents, a couple from church stopped by. Jay had been a pastor for just five years or so, and I was doing my best to juggle the roles of pastor's wife and mom to three kids under the age of six. Garry and Carol had been running errands, and they felt like the Lord told them to drop by on their way home to see how we were doing. In fact, I'm sure it was the Lord's prompting, because Jay and I were fighting, and there's no way we would have invited them over to see *that*.

Now you need to know me and my sweet man to truly grasp the nature of our "fights." We're not screamers, though once in a blue moon we will raise our voices. We don't throw things either. (We made this rule after I accidentally gave my husband a black eye during a heated argument just after our first anniversary, when I kicked my shoe off at him and it hit him squarely in the eye. It was totally an accident, but he's still getting marriage mileage from it!)

It's embarrassing to admit, but that day we were pretty up in arms over a parenting issue with one of our delightful little angels. I can't remember what it was about—when you have seven kids, those details can get a bit fuzzy—but I'll never forget the humbling experience of looking at our screen door and seeing Garry and Carol standing there staring at us . . . and looking rather amused. After all, it's not every day you happen to walk in on your pastor and his wife acting like three-year-olds in a sandbox.

"Is this a bad time?" Carol asked, sheepishly holding out a box of doughnuts.

Jay and I looked at each other. I felt my face getting hot. "Of course not," we lied. "Come on in."

Garry and Carol sat on the couch, but the awkwardness of the moment persisted. Finally, I looked at Jay and then back at our friends. There was no point in pretending that now was a "good time." We were clearly not having a great day.

"To be honest," I started, "we're having a disagreement. Do you mind if we get your perspective on it?"

It's worth noting here that Garry and Carol weren't a couple of newlyweds. They were the parents of five wonderful daughters, and we had a tremendous amount of respect for them. We were still very much in the "experimental" part of our parenting, and we clearly needed some advice and godly counsel.

Carol and Garry spent quite a while listening to us talk about our problems and a *particularly* long time patiently sitting by as I unpacked a load of my insecurities about motherhood. That's when Carol noticed something.

"Heidi, I see you've been reading a lot about parenting," she said. She was right. On the coffee table in front of them sat a plethora of books. Carol picked up one of my favorites and thumbed through it. "This is a pretty good one," she said as she put it back on the table, "but I can't help noticing the absence of the book you *really* need to be reading."

I raised an eyebrow. *Good!* I thought. She was going to lead me to the holy grail of parenting books! I reached for a pen and paper.

"I don't see a Bible anywhere on this table."

(Insert painful silence here.)

I'm not gonna lie: that was awkward. Here I was, a pastor's wife, caught in a full-on argument with my husband, surrounded by every self-help book on the shelf . . . *except* the Bible.

Great.

Now Carol wasn't being rude; her tone wasn't the least bit condescending. I knew she loved me. I also knew she was right.

"Heidi," she continued, "if you commit to spending more time in your Bible, you will soon discover that you won't need to rely on these other books. The Bible and the Holy Spirit are all you really need. Wisdom starts in the Word. God will give you whatever else you are lacking. And if that includes finding encouragement from these other books, you'll know that, too."

It's been nearly twenty years since then, but I've never forgotten Carol's exhortation to me. It was the first time that I realized I was depending on human voices and that those voices were taking priority over the voice of my heavenly Father.

To be MomStrong is to understand what comes first. Our priority must be hearing from the Lord in every aspect of our lives. If we're not listening for the still, small voice of the Holy Spirit, we're more likely to fall victim to the latest and greatest parenting fad or to get sucked into the trap of believing we can do it without the Lord—and that's exactly what the enemy wants.

THE TROUBLE WITH COOKIE-CUTTER PARENTING

Garry and Carol's visit marked the beginning of when Jay and I turned away from cookie-cutter parenting advice and started learning to listen more carefully for God's wisdom. Good teachers and pastors are wonderful, but they're no substitute for time alone with the Lord. We need to hear from God more than we hear from people.

In the nineties, Jay and I participated in a popular parenting class at our church with several other young couples. Those were formative years for all of us, and we wanted to get it right. All the parents who took the class with us were well meaning, and I'm sure the author of the course was well meaning too. But the results (i.e., how the theory worked in real life) ranged from disappointing to devastating. The problem? Too many of us accepted this cookie-cutter approach to parenting as the inspired Word of God rather than directly seeking the Lord.

We all did our best to follow the advice laid out in the book we were studying. It touched on virtually every aspect of parenting: there was a right way and a wrong way to feed babies, and there was a right way and a wrong way to do naptime and bedtime. It really was a formula for parenting. The trouble is, formulaic approaches to parenting don't usually work, because each child is different. We learned very quickly that what worked for one child didn't necessarily work for the next one, and so on.

Many of the lessons we learned in the class were excellent, but the hard-and-fast rules of the program set the stage for what turned into legalistic, performance-based parenting. It was as if there were a competition between the families in the class. Whose kids were the most polite? Which ones came running as soon as they heard their names?

One morning in church, I noticed that my kids were arguing over something. Normally I would have just corrected the situation, but in this parenting competition I'd placed myself into, the stakes seemed higher. I felt like I had to crack down hard on the infraction. Suddenly I felt like everyone was watching my children. It didn't help that I was a pastor's wife either. Every time the kids disobeyed me in church, I was deeply embarrassed for others to view my apparent lack of parenting know-how.

The comparison trap was stealing the joy from parenting—but worse than that, it had us all focused on achieving temporary obedience rather than gaining insight into our individual children. That pride and embarrassment put the focus solely on my children's *actions* rather than on their hearts.

This is the real danger of formulaic parenting. Formulas tend to make parents believe that correct actions always indicate a contrite heart. Of course, that's simply not true. A child can be made to sit down on the outside and still be standing on the inside. In the past twenty years, I've never met a mom who merely wanted her children to *act* like good kids. We want more than that for our kids—we want them to *be* good kids. Unfortunately, performance-based parenting often encourages just that—a performance.

> *Performance-based parenting often encourages just that—a performance.*

Of course, reading advice from other godly people isn't bad; we can glean much wisdom from believers who have walked the journey before us. But when we do all our learning from others and forget to spend time with the Lord, we're in danger of winning the battle and losing the war.

The battles come in the form of everyday issues like getting your kids to put away their toys, sit still at the dinner table, and brush their teeth. These are largely just prewar warmups, and we all approach these situations differently. But *war* is different: the stakes are higher. We're talking about the hearts and minds of our children here—their character, their compassion, their moral foundation, and their capacity to love. Matters of preference are inconsequential; matters of the heart and soul are eternal. MomStrong moms understand the difference, and while they don't ignore the battles, they know that their primary focus must be on winning the war.

MomStrong moms don't ignore the battles, but they know that their primary focus must be on winning the war.

WHEN FATHER DOESN'T KNOW BEST

I want to go a little deeper with this "battle vs. war" idea because I know firsthand how easy it is to lose sight of the larger goal of capturing the hearts of our children. It's possible to win battles with our kids over lesser things but lose their hearts in the process. To that end, MomStrong moms are always asking, "What's the bigger issue?" It's easy to look back and agree that having a kid who isn't potty trained by the time the books say he should be pales in comparison to making sure the hearts of our children are tuned to hear that still, small voice of the Lord. The hearts of our children are what we want to guard above all else, and perhaps no one learned this lesson the hard way as much as King David did.

In 1 Kings 1:1-14, we read the story of King David and two of his sons, Adonijah and Solomon. Both his sons knew their father was dying, and both wanted to be king in his place. As we read the story, we see that Adonijah was absolutely set on taking his dad's place, despite the fact that the throne had already been promised to Solomon. Adonijah began boasting, "I will make myself king!" He then got together a bunch of chariots and chari- oteers and recruited fifty men to run in front of him (see 1 Kings 1:5). According to Scripture, King David had never disciplined his son at any time, even by asking, "Why are you doing that?" (see 1 Kings 1:6).

Seriously? *Never?* Listen, I wasn't there (I know—shocker), but my guess is that King David's children were not all that unlike my own kids. I bet they pushed their parents to the abso- lute limit dozens of times. In fact, I'm sure they gave their father dozens of reasons to discipline them, but even so, the Bible says King David didn't take advantage of any of these opportuni- ties. David gave Adonijah autonomy, position, and everything money could buy, yet he neglected to give him the one thing he needed most: fear and respect for the Lord.

So how'd *that* work out? Well, to make a long story short, while Adonijah was running around partying with his friends and anointing himself king, David followed through on his promise to his wife Bathsheba and anointed their son, Solomon, king instead. When Adonijah tried to overtake his brother's throne, Solomon had him killed. And there you have it: a seri- ous case of winning a battle and losing a war. David's failure to hold his sons accountable for their actions cost both him and his family dearly.

There is a huge part of me that totally gets what David was going through. Like most parents, I imagine that David probably got tired of listening to complaints from and about his children. After all, King David had many wives—there are eight named in the Bible. The man had his hands full, with nineteen sons and at least one daughter. He had a full-time job just managing the people of Israel, let alone all his wives and children.

It would be easy to make excuses for David's lousy track record, but instead I hope we can learn from it. First lesson: just say no to multiple wives. And on a more practical level, even when we feel overwhelmed by the job of correcting our children—when we think we can't do it for one more second—our kids need us to stay engaged. David's decision to disengage from the hard work of parenting left his family tree in chaos.

The way I see it, David's troubles aren't that different from our own. (Well, with the exception of the multiple wives. Even *I* can see that's a bad idea.) Regardless, our culture today is quick to excuse parents from the tough job of parenting.

In February 2013, police officers pulled over fifteen-year-old Ethan Couch in the family pickup truck. In addition to having no driver's license, the underage Texan boy was drunk on vodka, an open bottle tossed in the back of the truck. A passed-out girl slumped next to Ethan in the passenger seat. It was widely reported that the young man was disrespectful to the police officer, who tried to warn him about the dangers of drinking and driving.

When Couch left later with his mother, Tonya, he had

received two citations for his crimes. This wasn't new territory for the Couch family, as they already had a history of defying the law and then using their wealth to avoid prosecution.[1]

Four months later on June 15, Ethan, drunk once again, plowed through a group of people helping at the scene of a minor accident. Four people were killed. In the court case that followed, Couch was charged with four counts of intoxication manslaughter and two counts of intoxication assault. Tarrant County prosecutors were seeking a maximum sentence of twenty years of imprisonment for Couch, but in December 2013, Judge Jean Hudson Boyd sentenced Couch to ten years of probation after his attorneys successfully argued that the teen needed rehabilitation instead of prison.[2]

While the story of Ethan Couch is tragic, it was his defense strategy that made his case famous. According to psychologist G. Dick Miller, who testified in court, Ethan was a product of "affluenza" and was unable to link his actions with their consequences because his parents had taught him that wealth buys privilege.

Does that sound like anyone else you know? If King David were alive today, I imagine his attorneys might have used a similar defense for his son. Blame belongs to the rich dad, overwhelmed with his own life, who by design or accident taught his kids that they didn't have to be responsible for their actions.

It's easy to think we are loving our children when we let them get away with wrong, but the opposite is true. Oh, how the outcomes for both of these families would have changed had they known, taught, and applied God's Word in their parenting decisions! Is it a guarantee of success? No. I know many wonderful parents whose children have chosen to walk away from their parents' godly instruction. But we aren't responsible for the outcome. As parents, we're accountable for training our children in righteousness. The results are up to God.

Parenting is a tough job, but thank God, we don't have to rely on our own wisdom. God has already given us the best parenting manual in the world—His Word. The more we teach our children to follow in the ways of the Lord, the better equipped they will be to face the challenges ahead and "be successful in all [they] do and wherever [they] go" (1 Kings 2:3).

I'M NOT GONNA LIE . . .

Let's be honest here. We can't give our children what we don't have ourselves. We can't train them in discipline and biblical values if we aren't living out those values in our own lives. And the truth is, our kids aren't the only ones who need help navigating the treacherous currents of modern society; we as parents are surrounded by lies too. We're being told that unborn babies have no right to life. We're being told that marriage between a man and a man or between a woman and a woman is not only okay, it's to be celebrated. Deception and unbiblical thinking have become so commonplace that we're afraid to even speak the truth for fear of being discriminated against or being labeled "intolerant."

What was once regarded as a parent's responsibility is now seen as an infringement on the child's rights. For example, parents today are being told that kids as young as elementary school age can make their own decisions about everything from birth control to which gender they want to be. We're being told that our children have the right to get an abortion without parental consent. Simple tasks like looking at your thirteen-year-old's medical records now require permission from your teenager! The assault on parental authority is no longer hidden in the shadows.

Today's parents can see trouble on the horizon, but they've been told to be quiet, to "live and let live." It's a dangerous ideology, because it keeps the truth concealed.

So what do we do?

Parents need wisdom and discernment in order to make the right decisions for their children. But where can we look to find it? Unfortunately, we can't even assume that our churches will lead us there. Every day it seems that more and more church leaders are laying aside the truth of God's Word and exchanging it for the lie that we can take God out of our everyday lives. In a misguided attempt to be loving, many Christians today—even pastors—are sacrificing truth for the sake of "love." But is it really loving to disregard the truth? The Bible says the two must never be separated—and yet many teachers and Christian leaders today would challenge this most basic of Christian teachings.

Recently, in a heartbreaking departure from biblical truth, former pastor Rob Bell teamed up with Oprah Winfrey to spread a message of equality and love. With her sights set squarely on the Christian community, Oprah interviewed Mr. Bell with the skill of a master marksman. When pressed by Oprah to explain when the church was going to "get" gay marriage, Bell replied, "We think it's inevitable and . . . we're moments away [from the church accepting gay marriage]." He went on to say, "The church will continue to be even more irrelevant when it quotes letters from two thousand years ago as their best defense."[3]

When I heard these words, my heart broke. Yet Paul warned us that this would happen. In 2 Timothy 4:3-4, he wrote: "A time is coming when people will no longer listen to sound and wholesome teaching. They will follow their own desires and will look for teachers who will tell them whatever their itching ears want to hear. They will reject the truth and chase after myths."

Likewise, the apostle Peter devoted most of 2 Peter to warning against false teachers:

> There were also false prophets in Israel, just as there will be false teachers among you. They will cleverly teach destructive heresies and even deny the Master who bought them. In this way, they will bring sudden destruction on themselves. Many will follow their evil teaching and shameful immorality. And because of these teachers, the way of truth will be slandered.
>
> 2 PETER 2:1-2

John, too, repeatedly warned of false teachers in his writings:

> Dear friends, do not believe everyone who claims to speak by the Spirit. You must test them to see if the spirit they have comes from God. For there are many false prophets in the world. 1 JOHN 4:1

Those "letters from two thousand years ago" that Bell views with such disregard are the very words of God. They are our best defense. In fact, they're our *only* defense! Without them, we are lost. God's Word doesn't change with the winds of the culture. His truth is eternal.

Scripture makes it clear that God's Word is true and unchanging:

> The sum of your word is truth,
>   and every one of your righteous rules endures forever.
>
> PSALM 119:160, ESV

When we stray from the Bible, we are in dangerous spiritual waters. MomStrong moms know the Word, and they respond to today's challenges with God-centered wisdom. Don't be deceived: your best defense, your only defense, is the Word.

MomStrong moms know the Word, and they respond to today's challenges with God-centered wisdom.

I've said it before, and I'll say it again: we can't give our kids what we don't have. If you aren't in the Word for yourself, you need to be—for your own sake as well as for the sake of your children. It's time we stopped leaning on our church leaders and religious figures to interpret the Bible for us and returned to reading it on our own—and not just on Sundays. God offers a promise for those who seek wisdom: they will find it. The war may feel long and fierce, but we don't have to go it alone:

Don't turn your back on wisdom, for she will protect you.
Love her, and she will guard you.
Getting wisdom is the wisest thing you can do!
And whatever else you do, develop good judgment.

PROVERBS 4:6-7

MOM**STRONG** MOM, SEEK HIS WISDOM

Becoming MomStrong means digging into God's Word for answers to the daily challenges you and your family face. If you've never done that before, I encourage you to do something that took me years to do—be intentional about making time to read the Bible each day, even if it's only a little bit at a time.

It's okay to start small. Commit to reading the Bible for just ten minutes each morning, and you'll be amazed at what you'll learn about the character of God and His heart for this hurting world. You'll also see that God has set standards in place since the creation of the world. His law is as steadfast as the law of gravity—and things go better when we obey, just as they do when we respect the laws that govern the physical world.

If you're struggling with one of your children or with a situation one of your children is facing, it's time to get on your knees and ask God for unique wisdom and perspective. God knows exactly what's going on, and He can give you the wisdom you need. Isn't that amazing? It's one of the reasons we have hope as Christian moms. Instead of facing all the challenges and changes of motherhood on our own, we have the Creator Himself walking alongside us.

PRAYER POINTS FOR A
BATTLE-READY MOM

- Pray that you will have clarity as you make parenting decisions (see James 1:5).
- Pray that your children will become wise and learn to love God's Word (see Psalm 119:105).
- Pray for wise mentors for you and your children (see Proverbs 15:22).
- Pray that, unlike King David, you will stay engaged with your children in every stage of their lives (see 1 Kings 1:1-14).

HISTORY IN THE MAKING

I have been homeschooling my kids for almost two decades now, and we have an art/music/library/spare room that also functions as a schoolroom. Taped around the room, near the ceiling, there is a time line of world history. I got the idea from my friend Suzy. When I was living in a small town just north of Seattle, Suzy was the envy of every homeschooling mom I knew. Everything she did was a-ma-zing. She was the original Pinterest mom. So when she said she was going to make a history time line for her kids, I thought, *Great idea! I'll do that too!* She graciously invited me over to her house to take a look at what she'd done.

Within a few minutes of arriving in her schoolroom, I wished I'd stayed home. Her time line was the *Mona Lisa* of time lines. It was a full-scale wall mural, and it looked like something out of Pottery Barn: Homeschool Edition.

Mine? Not so much. Maybe it was because I was pregnant with my fourth child at the time, but I wasn't going for a Pottery Barn look so much as for finished. With this simple goal in mind, I purchased some white 8½-by-11 card stock and ran it through our printer so we'd have a line to work off of. After that, I taped all the pages together and secured them with pushpins around the room. The minimalist in me won the day. It wasn't perfect, but it was done.

That was seventeen years ago. Today the tape is yellowed and the ink is fading, but if you can look past the part where our parrot gnawed holes from 1600 to 1890 and see beyond the coffee stains near the life of Florence Nightingale, you might still appreciate our simple, tattered attempt at understanding all the extraordinary events we'll never be able to witness ourselves. It's no Sistine Chapel ceiling, but it tells a story just the same.

My husband and I have always explained to our children that history is something worth digging into, because history is more than just a series of dates on a time line. History is really HIStory—God's story—the unfolding of the Master's plan. We get to witness only about .001 percent of it, but we can appreciate the rest through the rearview mirror.

There are a lot of important dates and people on our time line: the birth of Christ, the reign of Napoleon, the world wars, the Holocaust, and the great revivals. Look closer and you'll see images of Beethoven, missionary Gladys Aylward, and President Ronald Reagan. There's even a little sticker that celebrates the birth of the United States.

And in 1967, nestled between the appointment of the first African American Supreme Court justice and the assassination of Senator Robert Kennedy, God did something amazing in the life of the St. John family. In 1967, God decided it was time for Jay St. John to become part of HIStory. And so, on a cool October day, Jay was born into the care of his mom and dad, Lou and Jerry St. John. Not too much later, in 1970, God determined that it was time for me to become part of HIStory. In 1989, our two lives became one, and HIStory continued to unfold as we became parents ourselves.

We have learned a lot together in our little schoolroom, but one of the most important things I want our children to know is the role they play in God's story. God's purposes are eternal, and each child He gives us has been born, like Esther, "for just such a time as this" (Esther 4:14). I want each of my seven children to know that God put them on this earth with a unique purpose. Their births were no less significant in God's economy than the birth of George Washington or Elisabeth Elliot. Their lives are precious, and I want them to know why. I want our children to learn about men and women who followed God throughout history (as well as about those who rejected Him), because I want them to see that they are just as much a part of God's story as anyone else whose picture graces our worn-out time line.

A WARRIOR IS BORN

So why tell you about my tattered and yellowed time line? Because in order for us to train our children for their own journeys of faith, we need to see ourselves on the continuum of HIStory. God is always at work, and He has placed you right here, right now, for such a time as this—to help prepare your children for the war that lies ahead!

Make no mistake: in the midst of homework assignments, chores, and the seemingly mundane conversations you have every day with your children, you are preparing warriors—warriors who will be asked to answer the tough questions culture is asking, asked to give an answer for the hope that lies within them (see 1 Peter 3:15). You are preparing warriors who at some point will be asked to choose between following God's law and following the culture. And in order to prepare warriors, you have to become a warrior yourself.

Most moms aren't warriors by nature . . . unless you mess with their babies.

If you've never thought of yourself as a warrior, it's okay. Most moms don't come into motherhood thinking they're enlisting for battle. Mothers are life givers. We're nurturers. We plan meals and put on Band-Aids and give hugs.

Most of us aren't warriors by nature . . . unless you mess with our babies. Am I right? Mess with a mama's babies, and you'll see a warrior born right before your eyes! But for the most part, we are unintentional warriors—we fight not by choice but by necessity. Make no mistake: we are at war. We're at war with a culture that blurs the lines between right and wrong, a culture that devalues the sanctity of human life, a culture that marginalizes the family values God put in place. In short, we're at war with the enemy of our souls. We're at war with the one the Bible teaches has one purpose: "to steal and kill and destroy" (John 10:10). It's serious business, this job of training up the next generation.

A MomStrong mom understands that she is a warrior, not just for her kids, but for the generations that follow. Even more important, because she sees herself as a warrior, a MomStrong mom is willing to fight for what God says is worth fighting for. She uses the sword of truth to cut a swath through the lies of the enemy. The apostle Peter tells us exactly who this enemy is: "Stay alert! Watch out for your great enemy, the devil. He prowls around like a roaring lion, looking for someone to devour" (1 Peter 5:8).

If we're going to raise a generation of strong children, we must learn to engage our enemy rather than run from him. The good news is that although Satan is a powerful adversary, God is mightier still. If we remain alert and walk in a right relationship with God, we will always have the upper hand over our enemy.

A MomStrong mom is willing to fight for what God says is worth fighting for.

One of my favorite verses in the Bible is Zephaniah 3:17. In it, the heart of our Father is seen so clearly:

The Lord your God is living among you.
    He is a mighty savior.
He will take delight in you with gladness.
    With his love, he will calm all your fears.
    He will rejoice over you with joyful songs.

This verse has been such a comfort to me as I have come to know my Savior. In my own journey to becoming MomStrong, I've realized that I can trust God even in the midst of a fierce battle. He is aware of the struggles we face. His heart is for us.

MomStrong moms know that they are engaged in a battle, but they don't let the fear of the battle distract them from the truth. They know that their children need to see that their mom trusts God no matter what happens in this life.

Precious mom, God understands the magnitude of the struggle you are facing, and He wants you to trust Him even as you raise your children in a frightening world. So take courage! God has already let us know exactly what we can expect from Him as we face trials and struggles. I've personalized Zephaniah 3:17 below:

- To the mom who feels abandoned, God says, "I am living among you."
- To the mom who is battle worn, God says, "I am your mighty Savior."
- To the mom who wonders if she is enough, God says, "I delight in you."
- To the mom who is afraid, God says, "Lean in to Me. I will quiet you with My love."
- And to the mom who has never felt the affirmation of an earthly dad, God says, "I rejoice over you with singing."

No matter what we face, God will give us the sustaining grace we need. He will never leave us or forsake us. He never has, and He never will.

WHEN YOU FEEL LIKE YOU'RE FAILING . . . LOOK UP

Not long ago, I was speaking about motherhood at a conference in Virginia. After three days of back-to-back sessions, I could feel myself getting tired. Jay and I had taken our kids with us for the speaking season, and this was the next-to-last stop on our four-month trip. Let me tell you, the grace was running out. Everyone was just getting on everyone else's nerves.

Shortly before I went on stage, I took our kids to the green-room to make sure everyone had their lunch. The greenroom was about a ten-minute walk from where I was going to speak, and the walk included an escalator. I hate those things—they attract kids like an incandescent light attracts mosquitoes. I have more than twenty-six years of parenting under my belt, and I have yet to find a cure for the siren song of the escalator.

As we were making our way to the greenroom, I gave this word of caution: "If you play on the escalator, there will be huge consequences later!" Not a particularly eloquent (or specific) threat, but it was the best I could muster up after four months away from home. And because my word is law, they all naturally decided they needed to jump off the final step "one more time."

Our fifth child was the last one to jump from the moving stairs of death. I watched as she catapulted her five-foot frame several feet into the air from the second step. Midway into her disobedient jump, her arm connected with the railing and she screamed. I suppose a good mom would have been concerned about an injury. Not me—I was just mad. I know, you wish I were raising your children.

"Mom! My hand hurts!" Summer wailed.

By this point, however, I was immune to wailing. As it

happens, my mom was a pediatric nurse, so I took a lesson from her playbook: I glanced at my daughter's hand and very matter-of-factly said, "Looks fine to me. Now stop crying and finish your sandwich." And then, just in case I didn't appear callous enough, I threw in a final "That's what you get for playing on the escalator."

I was so irritated! Here I was, getting ready to speak in front of a standing-room-only crowd—on parenting, mind you—and I couldn't get my own children to obey one simple request. I was so distracted by my circumstances that I forgot to gird up for battle. I forgot to pray. I let my flesh overpower my spirit, and do you know what I heard whispered in my heart the entire time I was speaking?

You're failing. You can't even get your own children to obey.

If these moms knew what you were really like, they would get up and leave.

You're a bad mother. You don't have anything to say that's worth hearing.

I fought for every single word that came out of my mouth that afternoon. No one seemed to know it, but I was in a full-blown war up there onstage. The voice of condemnation that spoke to my soul was almost audible, and it threatened to undo me.

Have you ever heard that voice? You don't need to be a public speaker to hear it. The devil knows his audience, and he knows our weak spots. His goal? To cloud our vision long enough that we lose sight of the true fight.

As long as we live on this earth, the voices clamoring to fill our souls with condemnation will persist. Weary, worn-out mothers are perfect targets for the enemy, and I was ripe for the picking that afternoon. You see, Satan is a master at making us believe that someone else could do our job better than we can. He knew exactly how to get to me that day, and he used my bad day to make me feel like a bad mom.

At that moment, I had a choice to make: I could accept the lies of the enemy and see myself through the eyes of the accuser of my soul, or I could see myself through the eyes of my Jesus.

When the session ended, I made my way to the back of the stage and found a quiet place to pray. Sometimes prayer doesn't seem as active as *doing* something, but in reality, there is nothing more powerful than bringing our whole selves to the Lord in prayer. God says that when we pray, He literally bends down to listen (see Psalm 116:2). That's my Jesus. That's my Savior.

Even today, tears fill my eyes as I remember His gentle words to me that day: *You are loved.* Loved when I lose my temper. Loved when I don't meet someone else's expectations for me, and loved when I do.

Bad days do not make bad moms.

Precious mom, don't let the enemy lie to you! If you believe the lies, you'll be right where he wants you. Bad days do not make bad moms. God wants us to know His joy when we have good days—and He wants us to experience His grace when we don't.

When we are assaulted by lies, we need to remember what and who we're fighting for. Some days our biggest fight will be to see ourselves as God sees us. Because if God is for us (which He always is), no one—not even Satan himself—can stand against us (see Romans 8:31).

THE LAUNCH CODE

Near the end of his life, Paul wrote, "I have fought the good fight, I have finished the race, and I have remained faithful" (2 Timothy 4:7). Paul considered his mission a battle to fight, a course to complete, and a commitment to keep. That's how I see motherhood. Like Paul, we mothers have a commitment to God, to our children, and to countless generations yet to come.

Paul tells us that the battle we're in is not against flesh-and-blood enemies (see Ephesians 6:12). It's a spiritual battle, and our families are right in the middle of it. A trained warrior notices when the landscape of battle changes, and she adjusts her tactics to meet the changing landscape, always keeping the end goal in sight.

There's no question that the spiritual landscape of our world is changing. As Christian mothers, our end goal is to train up a generation of strong, Christ-centered adults who can use the Word of God wisely and who faithfully discern the truth for themselves.

If we're going to follow Paul's example and finish well, we need to remain strong. Psalm 127:4 says, "Like arrows in the hands of a warrior are children born in one's youth" (NIV). I love the powerful imagery of this verse. There is a battle going on, and as parents, we are warriors in it. The Bible says that our children have been given to us "like arrows in the hands of a warrior."

Several years ago, my friend Ann Dunagan heard me speak at a conference in South Carolina. I was talking about this passage, urging moms to see their roles not as passive but as active.

When I read this psalm's description of the warrior, I described two warrior-parents working in harmony with each other as an illustration of how we are to raise our children.

The following year, I saw Ann again at a conference in our home state of Oregon, and her son Mark was with her. Mark had something for me—something I treasure to this day. He had created a sculpture based on this verse. The sculpture has two figures, a man and a woman, both in medieval armor.

As I looked at the sculpture, the verse came alive to me in a way that's hard to capture in words. The sculpture depicts my husband, Jay, standing just in front of me, shield up and sword drawn. Several black arrows have attempted to penetrate the shield he's holding. His stance is strong and protective, but the woman behind him isn't just standing there. Under the protection of her husband, the woman, a skilled archer herself, is launching her own arrows with steely-eyed determination. There are seven arrows depicted—representing our seven children—one arrow in my bow and six in our quiver.

Surely we were born for this—to launch our arrows into the world for the Kingdom of God!

To this day, I keep Mark's sculpture prominently displayed in our home. What a beautiful picture of God's design for marriage and the family! To me it says, "This is worth fighting for." Surely we were born for this—to launch our arrows into the world for the Kingdom of God!

MOMSTRONG MOM,
KNOW WHAT YOU'RE FIGHTING FOR

If you're not sure what your role in the battle is or which battles are worth fighting, ask God to give you insight into the hearts of your children. Be aware of the influence you have in their lives as you teach and nurture them, and don't let the enemy divert you from your mission. A mom who is sure of her course and her calling isn't easily swayed by the opinions or comments of others. Remember, you're fighting for your children and your children's children. You're fighting to uphold the legacy of strong, God-honoring warriors that began in the book of Genesis and that will continue for generations to come! This is *your moment* on the time line. Never forget: God has placed you here for such a time as this.

Just like the archer in Psalm 127, there will come a time to let your arrows fly. If your heart is focused on the big picture of raising godly children, it will be easier to strengthen your grip on the bow and steady your stance. Releasing arrows into the world isn't for the faint of heart, but MomStrong moms know when it's time to let their children go. They don't hold on to them out of fear but instead move forward with the holy determination that comes from living in the light of God's Word. We must aim our arrows carefully, releasing them only when our aim is sure and our arrows are ready to fly. After all, when an archer is in battle, she doesn't get two tries with the same arrow. She gets only one. Make sure you make yours count.

PRAYER POINTS FOR A
WARRIOR-IN-TRAINING MOM

- Pray that God will protect you from believing the enemy's lies and that you will embrace His truth instead (see John 8:44).
- Pray that God will prepare your children for each battle they face (see Ephesians 6:10-18).
- Pray that you will release your "arrows" into the world at the right time, in the right way (see Psalm 127:4).

Chapter 3

FACING YOUR GIANTS

I learned something new about arrows a few years ago, when Cupid fired an arrow smack into the heart of our oldest daughter, Savannah. I thought seeing our kids graduate from high school and go out into the world was hard, but it paled in comparison to the day Savannah got married.

Actually, let me back up a little. The wedding day itself was easy. In fact, it was glorious. Watching my daughter become a wife under the willow trees near our home, surrounded by our dearest friends and family, was a beautiful culmination of years of prayers, tears, and hopes—once my heart made the transition, that is.

What is it with transitions? First it's childbirth, and then . . .

well, it's the rest of your life. Motherhood is all about learning and change, isn't it? God uses each new phase to grow us up while we try to help our children grow. Such a grand paradox!

When my daughter got engaged, I got a lesson on letting go. At twenty, Savannah was a beautiful young woman who loved and served the Lord. She had met and fallen in love with a wonderful young man who also loved the Lord. That was good, right? Of course it was.

The trouble was, I forgot that I was launching an arrow, not throwing out a boomerang! You see, I was raised in a home filled with strife and domestic violence. As you might imagine, I had serious trust issues as a result. I struggled to trust my daughter with any man who was not named Jay St. John. In a misguided attempt to protect my daughter, I forgot that God could take better care of her than I ever could. Rather than take my fears to the Lord, I worried and fretted over her future. Even though Savannah had spoken to her dad and me about her desire to get married, I still struggled.

Shortly after Savannah and Ryan got engaged, I called our dear friends Steve and Jane Lambert. I desperately needed a sounding board, and thankfully I had the Lamberts, who have been like parents to me for many years.

"She's so *young*!" I lamented. (I seemed to have forgotten the fact that I was nineteen when I got married.) "They're not ready! What's the rush?"

Steve and Jane were quiet while I poured out my heart and my fears over the phone.

"Do you want my advice?" Steve finally asked.

"Yes," I replied sheepishly.

"Did you raise your daughter to hear from the Lord?"

"Yes."

"Then you need to let her hear from Him," he went on. "Do you trust God's heart for her?"

"Yes."

"Then it's time to let her follow God's leading. You need to trust that she's hearing from the Lord for her own life now."

Those last two sentences hit my heart hard. I could hear the Lord speaking through Steve. I knew I'd been holding on too tightly. My intentions may have been good, but I was wrong. Motherhood teaches us that we're wrong a lot, doesn't it?

> *Motherhood is all about courage, from the moment you watch your baby take those first wobbly steps.*

Even once I knew it was time to let her go, I struggled to be happy about it. Rather than rejoicing with my daughter, I became "that mom"—you know, the one we all made fun of before we had kids of our own. I knew I needed to shift my thinking. I needed to have God's perspective for our daughter. After all, it's always much better than my own!

Shortly after that phone call, Jay and I invited Savannah out to dinner, gave her our blessing, and told her we trusted in her ability to hear from the Lord. We also affirmed her choice.

An August wedding followed, and Savannah was right: Ryan is the perfect match for her. He brings a levity and joy to our family that we couldn't have imagined. Ryan and Savannah are off on their own wonderful adventure now. Their two sons are a delight to all of us—and we are richer for launching our arrow when the time was right.

Motherhood is all about courage, from the moment you watch your baby take those first wobbly steps. Many of the steps they'll take after that are wobbly too. The trick is to trust the Lord as you wobble through each transition together.

God has plans for your children, just as He has plans for you. But remember, we see only the tiniest fraction of God's grand design. That's why we need God's perspective for our children—it's the only one that really matters.

THE BEST-LAID PLANS

When it comes to making plans, I am second to . . . well, just One. Planning is in my DNA. I am a list maker and a lover of all things calendar related. Just give me an idea and a deadline, and I'll make it happen—that is, if only the universe would cooperate! I shudder to think of the thousands of my perfectly laid plans that have been completely derailed by everything from forgetting to plug in the slow cooker to getting in a fender bender on the way to the store.

The truth is, we can't plan for everything. And perhaps more to the point, no one ever plans for a crisis. We don't pencil in "crisis" on the third Monday of the month. And yet, without fail, with the bases loaded at the bottom of the ninth, the phone rings, and voilà—your child is sick, a family member has lost his job, a friend has devastating news. This is where courage needs to step up to the plate.

The Bible says that we can make our plans, but ultimately

the Lord determines our steps (see Proverbs 16:9). And some of those steps can be pretty painful to take. Having lost a baby to miscarriage and wept beside the casket of a dear friend's stillborn daughter, I know that we don't always get to choose what happens to the babies we carry so carefully inside us. We can't always predict what a day will bring. But we are guaranteed this: God will never leave us or forsake us (see Hebrews 13:5). Ever.

And oh, how we need Him! God is the One who brings courage in the chaos and peace to the broken places in our hearts. Without the courage that comes from God, a spirit of fear can settle into the unseen places of a mother's soul. So stay close to Him, precious mom! Get to know His Word. Memorize His promises. Don't let that fear take root.

Every mom can identify with fear, but every mom can also identify with the antidote to fear that we've been given. From the moment we know we're bringing a new life into the world, something miraculous—even sacred—awakens in the heart of a mother: courage.

It takes courage to be a mother. Unplanned C-sections, unexpected diagnoses, illnesses, sibling rivalry, bad attitudes, and strong-willed children test the courage and resolve of every mother. But God uses all of these circumstances to help make us into the mothers He wants us to be.

I know it's true, because this business of shaping little hearts is also shaping mine. Motherhood has exposed weaknesses in me I never knew I had, has driven me to the limits of what I thought I could do, and has filled my heart with hopes and dreams I never imagined for a future I can only entrust to God. There's no doubt about it: becoming a mother changes everything. And even twenty-six years in, I'm finding I need fresh courage on a daily basis.

Let's face it: this isn't our grandparents' generation. Choosing a Christ-centered life in a culture that rejects Christ is challenging the courage of many believers today. We are parenting in a generation in which fear is a driving force in our decisions. Standing for what the Bible says about marriage and human sexuality is growing increasingly unpopular as our culture moves away from the truth and toward moral relativism. As a result, Christian mothers today have to do something the previous three generations didn't have to worry about: we're preparing our kids to face rejection.

How do we do that? We teach our children that their true identity comes from the Lord. If we (or our children) base our identity on what others think of us, Satan can begin to tell us his lies the moment we feel the sting of disapproval. In this culture of "tolerance," we should expect to be rejected. The way of the Cross is to live in full view of the world but to keep our eyes on Jesus. If we're going to live counterculturally, we need to know who God says we are.

So what does God say about our identity?

- Because of God's great love for us, we have been adopted into His family (see 1 John 3:1) and made joint heirs with Christ (see Romans 8:17).
- We are made alive and united with Christ (see Ephesians 2:5-6).
- We are blessed with all spiritual blessings in Christ (see Ephesians 1:3).
- We are made right with God through faith in Christ (see Romans 3:22).

- We are entitled to a clean conscience before God because of Jesus (see Hebrews 10:22).
- Our sins have been removed from us as far as the east is from the west (see Psalm 103:12), and God doesn't remember our sin (see Hebrews 8:12).
- The same love that the Father has for Jesus Himself is now ours (see John 17:23).

UNCOMMON COURAGE

It takes courage to stand for the Lord in the face of rejection, but stand we must. The next time your children tell you they have been mocked or labeled for their faith or beliefs, remember that at the moment of our salvation, God Himself gave us an even more powerful label. We wear the label Redeemed, and no one can relabel us! We are forever accepted by God.

Courage is found where acceptance abounds: in Christ.

If you're struggling to find courage in the face of being rejected, look up—and point your children's gaze to Jesus as you do. Courage is found where acceptance abounds: in Christ. Our role in HIStory is no less significant than that of Joshua, who found supernatural courage from the Lord in the midst of overwhelming challenges. Listen to what God said to Joshua when he received the mantle of leadership from Moses and was charged with leading the Israelites into the Promised Land:

Be strong and courageous, for you are the one who will lead these people to possess all the land I swore to their ancestors I would give them. Be strong and very courageous. Be careful to obey all the instructions Moses gave you. Do not deviate from them, turning either to the right or to the left. Then you will be successful in everything you do. Study this Book of Instruction continually. Meditate on it day and night so you will be sure to obey everything written in it. Only then will you prosper and succeed in all you do. This is my command—be strong and courageous! Do not be afraid or discouraged. For the LORD your God is with you wherever you go.

JOSHUA 1:6-9

Mothers who possess the stand-up courage of Joshua are Spirit-filled women. They know who they are in Christ, and they refuse to allow the devil to lie to them. They rise to the challenge of the culture and, in the process, shape the hearts and minds of their children for the glory of God.

Yes, we are living in challenging times, but like Joshua, we have been called to "be strong and courageous." This is an exciting time to be a Christian, because when faith finds its feet in this generation of parents and their children, we are going to see amazing things happen in the lives of God's people.

FACING YOUR GIANTS

Of all the wonderful stories in the Bible, the story of David and Goliath remains one of my favorites. Just imagining David—a young boy—loading a small stone into a sling and stepping onto the battlefield in the name of the Lord strengthens my own resolve to be courageous.

The reality is that we all face different kinds of giants in our lives. The question isn't whether they'll show up; it's whether we'll have the courage to load our own stones into our own slings when the time comes.

Several years ago, I decided it was time to face a huge giant in my life. That giant's name was Fear. For me, facing this giant meant risking my reputation as a "put-together" mom, author, and speaker by sharing one of my most personal struggles: the childhood trauma I had faced, along with the years of crippling anxiety I had experienced as a result.

I'll never forget the first time I stepped onstage with the intention of telling the truth about this tender part of my life. I knew God had asked me to address the very real problem of domestic abuse within the church while speaking to a group of homeschooling women. The only way to do it with authority was to be honest about the abuse I had experienced growing up.

I prayed for weeks in advance about what I'd say, and every time I even thought about it, Fear (and his henchman, Adrenaline) would hijack my mind and my body. My hands got clammy, my heart raced, and my anxiety soared. But all the while, God was teaching me to recognize the spirit of fear and reminding me to remain in Him.

The day I took the stage to share what had previously been known only to close friends and family, it felt very much like I was picking up a stone and chucking it with all my strength at the giant that had held me hostage most of my adult life. Sometimes the only way to do something is to do it afraid.

Do you know what happened when I took aim at that giant?

God showed up. When I obeyed the Lord, something miraculous happened: He began to set me free. As I testified to God's unfailing love in the middle of my trials, I saw tears rolling down the faces of many of the women in the audience. The response was overwhelming.

That day I learned that the devil doesn't want us to share our struggles. He wants us to feel that we're all alone. Isn't that what the devil does best? He tries to keep us from knowing the truth. To my surprise, I was learning that I was far from alone in my struggle. God wanted to use my story, including the broken parts, even as I was still finding my own healing.

Sometimes the only way to do something is to do it afraid.

We all have different fears we battle. But one common characteristic of most fears is that they stem from the lies we believe. Maybe Satan has whispered some of these lies into your ears at some point:

- *You're not strong enough.*
- *Your past has determined your future.*
- *Everything depends on you.*
- *You've failed too many times.*
- *You can't do this right.*
- *You're screwing up your kids.*
- *Everyone else's kids are doing better than yours.*

When I say these statements out loud, I know they're lies, but somehow in the quiet of my heart, they sound different. They sound believable.

When I was a young mother, I struggled to differentiate between the voice of the enemy and my own insecurities. I had grown up hearing stories about the lineup of courageous people in the Bible. I knew all about Joshua and the battle of Jericho, I could tell you all the ways Mary was brave, and I could quote a whole bunch of verses about faith—but it was just "Christianese." I knew the stories of courage, but I couldn't translate them into power for my own life.

Can you relate? We need a giant-sized sling to face the giants in our own lives. Thankfully, God supplies slings when we ask Him to. He's good like that.

I know all this talk of courage can sound kind of cliché, so let me unpack it for you just a little. MomStrong moms recognize that courage isn't the absence of fear; it's the decision to act in the face of fear. When we face our fears in faith, what we're really doing is allowing the Holy Spirit to be what He says He is: bigger than our fears.

When we pick up our slings and take aim at our giants through the power of the Holy Spirit, our aim will be sure. Fear is no match for the Lord of heaven's armies. According to the Bible, God is pretty good at helping amateurs like David make their aim count. It took only one stone to bring down the Philistine giant.

The same is true for us. When our trust is in the Lord, courage finds its feet. My grandmother once said, "God is faithful, or He isn't. He's good, or He isn't." There's no such thing as halfhearted faith—we need to go all in. Our trials present us with opportunities to put feet to our faith.

My first real opportunity to face fear regarding one of my children came in May 1993. I was expecting our second baby, and Jay and I were filled with anticipation as we went to get a peek at our little one via ultrasound. We couldn't wait to see our baby's sweet silhouette on the screen and to hear a strong heartbeat on the monitor.

As the technician dimmed the lights and began to move the transponder over my belly, Jay and I stared in amazement at the black-and-white image that appeared before us. It was love at first sight. Each movement the baby made delighted us. We weren't even paying attention to the measurements. The only thing we knew was that this little one was meant for us. Perfectly formed. A miracle. Beautiful. Ours.

We'd already decided we didn't want to know the sex of the baby, so there wasn't a lot of back-and-forth between us and the technician, other than our occasional questions about what this or that was. After about twenty minutes, the technician turned off the ultrasound machine and asked us to go down the hall for a follow-up with our doctor.

In the hour that followed, we heard words that no expectant parents want to hear: our baby's measurements were "off." The doctor shared concerns about the size of what appeared to be a hole in our baby's heart. In addition, he told us that the femur measurements seemed to validate the results of the AFP test I'd had done a few weeks prior. Our baby was at "extremely high risk" of having Down syndrome—as well as a possible heart defect. Fear gripped my heart as I held Jay's hand.

We were referred to a genetic counselor and scheduled for another ultrasound at a hospital in Portland. The second ultrasound confirmed what the first one had indicated, but without an amniocentesis, there was no way to know for sure if our baby had Down syndrome. Without speaking, we walked from the ultrasound suite down the hall to see the genetic counselor. The wait was excruciating.

Finally, Jay and I sat in a consultation room, miles apart from each other at opposite sides of the table. The room felt cold and unwelcoming.

"I'm sorry," the counselor began. "I wish I had better news, but the fact is that we just don't know with certainty what is happening with the fetus. Several markers indicate Down syndrome, but without an amniocentesis, we won't know for sure."

I cringed. This was no fetus. Not to me! This was my baby. I could feel her kicking inside me. I marveled at the occasional hiccup and stray foot or elbow. Nevertheless, this baby had no real voice—except the one her father and I gave her that day.

After hearing the risks and the benefits of amniocentesis, and knowing that the baby might have a heart defect, we decided against stressing her heart with further, more invasive testing. This meant our options were limited to—and I quote—"abortion or wait and see."

Our choice to wait and see must have seemed like either uncommon courage or plain stupidity to the genetic counselors, but abortion was out of the question. This was our daughter, and we loved her. We left the hospital in an emotional and spiritual fog, but even in the midst of our fears, God met us. "Do not fear, for I am with you" (Isaiah 41:10, NIV). We just kept repeating the verse over and over and over.

There is power in the spoken word of God. Even as we

struggled to find our own words, God's Word gave us strength. He does not fail.

Over the next several months, friends and family joined with us to pray for our unborn child. We prayed for healing. We prayed for peace. And then we prayed some more. I'd like to tell you that I was able to just let it go, but I struggled. Daily. Each little kick reminded me that my child might enter into this struggling world with a struggle all her own. I cried out to God. I tried to enjoy the four remaining months leading up to her birth, and while I did experience moments of peace, my heart was still heavy.

Fear threatened to settle over me like a cold, wet blanket many times in those months. The stress was enormous . . . but the grace that covered us was bigger than our fear. In those months, I learned that God never wastes anything.

God's grace takes our fears and transforms them into the kind of courage that motherhood requires.

And that's what I want you to hear: God's grace is bigger than our fears. It's God's grace that takes our fears and transforms them into the kind of courage that motherhood requires. My grandmother was right. Either we would believe God or we wouldn't. Our resolve was tested, but we chose to believe that God's Word is true. We chose to believe our daughter's life belonged to God.

It wasn't until much later that I realized the real victory was found not in facing my fears or even in overcoming them. The real victory happened the day we chose life for our daughter, regardless of the outcome. When we chose life, we picked up our sling and looked our giant right in his wicked eyes. The victory began when we chose to obey in spite of our fear.

The victory begins when we choose to obey in spite of our fear.

When we chose life, we were saying, "I trust you, God." God was listening. We just didn't know it yet.

Sierra was born a few months later, on a cold December morning. The room was full of specialists. A team from the NICU joined us in the delivery room, and a heart doctor was on call. But more than that, God's grace was all over that room, and His peace flooded our hearts. In choosing life, we said to everyone who was watching that we valued what God valued. No matter the outcome, we loved our daughter. We saw her as a gift, and we praised God for her.

Sierra Marie St. John made her entrance into God's story right on time, and against the odds, she was perfect. I had never cried so hard before. Yes, there was fear, but God was also there—and He is much bigger and much more powerful than our fear. Where the hurt runs deep, the grace runs deeper.

Sierra is now a grown woman. In the years since she was born,

God has given us dozens of opportunities to pick up our slings and choose trust over fear, regardless of the circumstances.

MOM**STRONG** MOM, HAVE COURAGE!

Part of becoming MomStrong is embracing the fact that we are all loved by God and precious to Him. If you're struggling to find courage in the midst of a battle, it's okay. Our faithful God knows every part of you. He sees every hurt and knows every detail of the fears you're facing.

MomStrong moms have uncommon courage, because their courage comes from God Himself. Where God's love is found, His courage is not far behind, because the Word tells us that perfect love drives out fear (see 1 John 4:18).

A mom who is committed to living this life for the Lord does more than act in the face of her fear; she decides to act in a way that brings glory to God in the midst of it. How can we do that? Through praise. Whatever circumstances you find yourself in right now, praise God. Praise Him in your pain; praise Him through your fear.

Author Mary Anne Radmacher says, "Courage doesn't always roar. Sometimes courage is the quiet voice at the end of the day saying, 'I will try again tomorrow.'"[1] It's all right if you don't feel like roaring, as long as you know this one thing down to the deepest part of your being: you are loved, and love gives feet to courage. In fact, it's where courage begins.

It's love that gives a mother the courage to push one more time. It's love that stays up all night with a newborn. It's love that allows a toddler to fall and get back up again. And it's love that gives a mother the courage to release her child into a new season, even as she steadies herself.

Uncommon courage is God's gift to every fearful mom who decides she can take Him at His word, no matter what she is facing. Watch and see—He will prove Himself faithful.

PRAYER POINTS FOR A
COURAGEOUS MOM

- Pray that you will hold your plans loosely and embrace God's plans for your life (see Proverbs 16:9).
- Pray that you will have uncommon courage to face your challenges (see Joshua 1:9).
- Pray that your children will be courageous and use their slings to defeat the giants they're up against (see 1 Samuel 17).

NOTHING WORTHWHILE IS EASY

*N*ot long ago, I received a message from one of my favorite companies, Amazon, letting me know I could arrange to have toilet paper delivered to my house on a regular basis. Now I'm not going to lie to you: discovering I could "subscribe" to toilet paper was like winning the mommy lottery for me.

Once I learned I could subscribe to toilet paper, I began to sign up for other things too—paper towels, shampoo, toothpaste, diapers, laundry soap, coconut milk, and (my favorite) chocolate. Hey, a girl's gotta have some of that on hand for emergencies!

Amazon recently came out with a service called Prime Now. Keyword? *Now*. If I decide I need something from their ever-growing "now" store, I can pay for it, and it will be delivered in less than two hours. Two hours! (Thank goodness, because that two-day wait was getting excruciating).

My point is that this is brilliant marketing on the part of the online giant. They know their audience. Most of us don't like to wait. We want a new kid by Friday, and we want to live our best life . . . well, *now*.

The trouble is, the best things in life take time. And no one understands that better than mothers. For nine months, a mother waits. We wait for that first cry. We wait to count all ten fingers and all ten toes. We wait for that first tender touch. But oh, the wait is worth it, isn't it?

> *Through all the waiting, hoping, planning, worrying, praying, trusting, crying, and celebrating, we become the mothers God wants us to be.*

And that's just the beginning. As our children grow, we wait for other firsts: first words, first steps, the first day of school. As Christian moms, we wait for the day when our children accept Jesus as their Savior. We wait to see them own their walk with God. We wait and pray they will make choices that will honor God and His Word in their daily lives as they mature into adulthood.

Day by day, year by year, we watch our children slowly become the people God wants them to be. And in the process—through all the waiting, hoping, planning, worrying, praying, trusting, crying, and celebrating—we also become the mothers God wants us to be. In fact, motherhood is all about becoming.

When we become mothers, we surrender ourselves to the process of becoming. Some sacrifices are small: the right to privacy, the never-before-fully-appreciated full night's sleep, quiet time, that last bite of cake at the party, the little bit of "extra" money that you decide should go to braces instead of a new car (and yes, that's about what they cost).

Other sacrifices are harder to grasp. When we become mothers, we also surrender our emotions (who knew it was possible to love such a tiny human being so much?), our pride (earlier is better on this one, trust me), our control, our freedom, and even our bodies (I once calculated forty-one straight months when I was either an incubator or a milk factory)—all for the privilege of becoming and watching our children do the same.

Somewhere in the midst of our caring for infants, toddlers, tweens, and teens—in the up-all-night exhaustion that only a mother can truly appreciate—God carves out the hope and future that He promises in Jeremiah 29:11. It's a miracle, really.

But that's how He works.

CLEANUP, AISLE 5

Let's not kid ourselves, though. The journey can be tough. It's not always easy being stretched, shaped, and twisted—even when we know the end result is going to be amazing. Sometimes the process of becoming can be downright humbling, especially where children are concerned.

I started to grasp this concept when my oldest daughter, Savannah, was about three and our second born was just nine months old. It was the fall of 1994, and my friend Margaret called to inform me that all the cake-decorating tools were on sale at our local craft store. Now it's a truth universally acknowledged that moms don't just "go" anywhere. Car seats, diaper bags, sippy cups, strollers—I'm sure the early settlers packed less baggage for their journey west. So imagine how proud I was when I strapped our infant and toddler into the car in less than ten minutes! Okay, I confess it helped that my younger sister, Hilary, was staying over (mother's helper for the win!), but still . . .

We arrived at the craft store shortly after it opened. I glanced at the diaper bag to make sure my mommy arsenal was complete. Diapers? Check! Nursing pads? Check! Nursing cover? Check! Sippy cup? Check! Wet wipes? Check! Emergency stash of Goldfish crackers? Check! When I was confident nothing had been left to chance, my sister and I headed inside the store to meet Margaret.

The baby was in her car seat, and Savannah was walking quietly alongside me, and I was feeling rather triumphant. Someone had recently told me that having two kids would be challenging. I decided that poor mom must have had pretty hard kids, because I was doing just fine.

It didn't take long for Hilary and me to become completely lost in the cake-decorating aisle of Oregon Craft and Floral. It was glorious. So many cake pans! (This was a phase of motherhood when I was still baking cakes from scratch.) I was absolutely *killing it* at this mommy gig. Sierra was snoozing away in her car seat, and Savannah was . . . right here a minute ago.

In my cake pan–induced euphoria, I had apparently forgotten I had a second child. (Did I mention how quickly we'd loaded up the car?) It wasn't until I heard a noise behind me that sounded very much like splashing that I realized something was wrong. At first I didn't pay much attention, because like a good mom, I hadn't brought Savannah's sippy cup into the store. Therefore, there was nothing to spill. Not my circus, not my monkeys.

Only it *was* my circus, and by the time I realized it was my monkey, it was too late. To my horror, Savannah had wet her pants. In my haste to get out the door (again—cake pans, people), I had forgotten that all-important training diaper. I had also forgotten to take her to the potty when we arrived at the store. Yep, I was batting 0 for 2.

Here I was, in the middle of the cake-decorating aisle, with a two-year-old happily splashing in a puddle she made "all by herself." I could feel my face getting hot. I turned around to ask my sister for help, but she had made the wise decision to take the baby and head for the car (because, you know—*family*), leaving me red faced and alone to call for a janitor.

Before I hit the call button on the nearest pole, I looked at the shelves. Savannah had splashed the bottom third of the cake pan section. There was no way anything could be sold after that.

Dejected and embarrassed, I pushed the button and waited for Armageddon. After what felt like the longest minute of my life, a store clerk approached. "Can I help you?"

I hesitated. Maybe it would be better if I just said she wet her pants. But if I was going to be honest (that pesky Bible!), I had to explain the whole "puddle jumping" thing. So I quickly blurted out, "I am so embarrassed! I didn't know she was going to jump in the puddle!" After which I'm pretty sure I started crying.

"My puddle!" Savannah emphasized. Yes, dear. *We know.*

The clerk surveyed the carnage and awkwardly asked if I shopped there often. I'm sure he was trying to figure out how to avoid me next time. Then he made a radio call, and "Wet cleanup!" sounded over the intercom.

Shortly thereafter, a bucket of bleach water arrived on the scene, and another horrified mother brought me a roll of paper towels from the bathroom. When the manager arrived, I asked if they would like me to pay for the damaged goods. I wanted to evaporate. In the space of thirty seconds, I had gone from feeling accomplished and in control to being embarrassed and humiliated, standing on top of a mountain of pee-soaked paper towels. That's when the miracle happened.

The look in the manager's eyes was pure grace. Why? Because like me, she was also a mother, only she was a little bit further down the path than I was. She knew it could have been her. Shoot, at one point it probably was. She understood. There were no snide remarks. There was no eye rolling, no condemnation. Just grace and understanding. It was a sisterhood of toddlerhood.

> *Motherhood teaches you as much about yourself as you learn about your child.*

The manager graciously told me they would take care of the damage and asked if I needed any help out. By this time, she could see I needed all the help I could get! I don't remember how I made it to my car without fainting, but that's the day I knew what I was up against. Motherhood takes no prisoners. It's the ultimate in on-the-job training, and it teaches you as much about yourself as you learn about your child.

My training in potty training wasn't yet complete (I needed boys to do that!), but after that fateful morning, I never again forgot to take training pants and a change of clothes. And do you know what else? From that day forward, I also became much more aware of other moms around me who were in the process of becoming. The mom who brought me a week's worth of paper towels from the store bathroom said it all with one glance, as did the store manager with her lack of condemnation: grace. They understood. And now so did I.

I think it's interesting to note that when God called Mary to embark on her unconventional motherhood journey, He sent her to an older, wiser woman—her relative Elizabeth. Mary didn't spend those first few months of parenting with her fiancé or with a parenting textbook; instead, she got some one-on-one mentoring from someone who was a few steps ahead of her in life and in motherhood (see Luke 1:39-45).

That seems like a pretty good model for us to follow. Sometimes we're the younger woman, gleaning wisdom from those who have gone before us, and sometimes we're the older woman, extending grace to moms who are newer at this gig. We need to be reminded that none of us "arrive" when it comes to motherhood. We are all in the process of becoming.

I've been doing this mothering thing for a while now, but the memory of the cake-pan-aisle walk of shame is still fresh in my mind. The only difference is that now I can laugh about it. (I recovered after about six months.) And I can assure you, there have been many more embarrassing, humiliating, and heartwarming escapades since that one. I'm still learning to roll with it, and sometimes I do better at that than other times.

Take, for example, our family outing to the pumpkin patch last October. Shortly after we got there, the trip became an epic, mud-soaked fail, so we piled into the van and went to our local grocery store, where we happily selected pumpkins and posed for pictures next to early Christmas displays. Fifteen years ago, I would have been disappointed. Now I'm just glad to have a few of my kids together to carve our pumpkins. It's all about perspective.

When you get down to it, new mothers and veteran mothers are basically the same. We all have the same struggles and insecurities. The only difference is that veteran moms have the gift of perspective. Veteran moms have weathered the storms of infancy, toddlerhood, and adolescence and have come out the other side wiser and more seasoned. They've experienced the challenges, anxiety, and fear, but they've also witnessed the triumphs, relief, and joy. Frankly, I'm grateful for the youthful enthusiasm of my oldest daughter, who is now a mom herself. She reminds me to delight in the little things.

We need each other, don't we?

MomStrong moms understand that motherhood is a journey and that becoming takes time. So the next time you see another mom struggling with a strong-willed toddler in the cereal aisle at the grocery store or gathering up a heap of urine-soaked paper towels at the craft store, try to remember that we've all been there (or easily could be someday).

And if you have chocolate or a gift card to your favorite local coffee shop, it might be a good time to pay it forward to a struggling mom in honor of the manager who cleaned up the cake-pan aisle after my child all those years ago. We moms have to stick together.

ARE WE THERE YET?

I think my husband and I have heard the phrase "Are we there yet?" from our children no less than seven million times. That's because we travel a lot as a family. I've been speaking to audiences around the world for about ten years, and for six of those, we've taken our children cross-country with us to build sibling relationships, develop character, and be together. (At least that's what we tell ourselves.) Trust me, we don't do it for the entertainment value or for the sheer convenience of it.

It's a do-or-die thing, these road trips we take. The last one was thirty-four thousand miles long. And believe me when I say there were many, many times on the road when nobody wanted to get there. We just wanted to *be* there.

The trouble is, no matter how much you want to be back in your own bed, no matter how tired you get of sitting in a van or sleeping in a cheap hotel room, you have to go the entire journey if you want to make it to your destination. You can't simply click your heels together and be anywhere you want to be.

And from my experience, shortcuts don't work either. Almost every time we tried to shave off time somehow, it ended in disaster. At the risk of bringing up an unpleasant experience for my kids (who will no doubt be dying to read their mom's book), I'll share about one trip in particular.

It was 2011, and we were quite literally near the end of the road in our third travel season. The conclusion we'd come to was that living with eight people in a twenty-nine-foot RV for four months straight makes you *really* miss your own bed.

We were winding our way through Wyoming near midnight when I noticed something bright flickering around the back of the RV on the driver's side. Sounds like a flame, doesn't it? But that wasn't all. The entire day, I'd been telling my road-worn, exhausted husband about a noise I was hearing near the rear of the RV. In our desperation to make it home, however, we kept ignoring it. Until the flickering.

As it turned out, the rear wheel bearings were as worn out as the passengers who were depending on them. And since we didn't pay attention to the signs, the tire overheated and caught on fire.

There's nothing quite like hearing your husband yell, "Get out! It's on fire!" as you unfasten sleeping children from car seats, grabbing blankets and shoes on the way. You can bet that as we stood on the side of the freeway watching fire trucks approaching from both directions, we wished we'd paid better attention to the signs.

Signs matter. We ignore them to our peril. We thought we'd save time in the short term and fix the problem when we got home. What we ended up with was a near-totaled RV, not to mention PTSD: road-trip edition, and a two-week extension of our trip while we waited for repairs. It would have been wiser to spend the time and money on a minor repair. Instead, we spent fourteen days and thousands of dollars more on a major one.

The lesson? As frustrating and painful as it may be, you just can't find a shortcut to the process of becoming. There's no way to get through motherhood without seeing the check engine light come on, and when it does, we're wise to pay attention. The truth is, it's easier to correct something if we can catch it early. Moms who notice that an attitude is a little off are wise to correct it before the attitude becomes an action or before an action becomes a habit.

There are no "now" apps to becoming MomStrong. It's all

about becoming, and when we try to shortchange the process, we lose out on the grace God offers.

GROCERIES AND UNGRACE

Have you ever experienced a lack of grace when it comes to motherhood? I have—in fact, I used to be on the giving end of that ungrace. Shortly after my husband and I graduated from a parenting class at our church (yes, I know—you can stop laughing now), I became convinced that I had this whole mothering thing figured out. I knew all the concepts of that class by heart. First-time obedience? Check! Respect for authority? Check! Feeding schedule? Check! Parent-led family? You know it.

I'm telling you, I was a pro. That whole cake-pan ordeal was now a distant memory, and I was sure I was up for some sort of mothering award. After all, I had four kids now, and not a single one of them had been the focus of a negative sermon illustration at the church where my husband served on the pastoral staff. Pretty good, right? What I didn't know was that I still had a lot to learn. Even four kids into my mothering journey, I was still very much a rookie at this whole gig. We'd been blessed with relatively easygoing kids, so it never occurred to me that parenting could get a lot more challenging. Now I know better.

One day I was in Walmart with my super-well-behaved examples of stellar parenting when I noticed that a toddler was beginning to give his mama a little trouble. I watched from behind the diaper aisle as the scene unfolded, and before too long, this kid was in full-on meltdown mode. His poor mother seemed at a total loss as to what she should do.

As the minutes dragged on, things only got worse. The child, who was clearly in control of the situation, got louder and more defiant. His mother, now totally humiliated, tried to stifle his screams as she hurried past the prying eyes of other shoppers. No one (myself included) made eye contact with her. She was an island.

As I pushed my cart in the opposite direction of the tyrannical toddler, I leaned in and whispered to my own daughter, "That child isn't practicing first-time obedience, is he?"

"No, Mama," came her wilted reply.

I'm embarrassed to admit it, but I actually thought, *I have a book for that mom,* as I watched her struggle to keep her child from totally losing it. I honestly thought that if this mom only knew what I, the great and powerful Oz of Motherhood, knew, she would not have a toddler problem at all. I was so wrong.

Oh, how I wish I had asked God to open the eyes of my heart in that moment! If I'd been looking at the situation with spiritual eyes, two things would have happened: I would have noticed my own sinful pride right away, and I would have been filled with grace for this mom. Why? Because I would have understood that it just as easily could have been me with the screaming toddler. Fortunately, God has profound ways of getting our attention.

Fast-forward two years. Same Walmart, different child. *My* child.

By now, I was a seasoned mother of five, walking down the diaper aisle with my children. We had officially entered the phase where, on every outing we took, heads turned in our direction. After all, it's not every day that you see a pregnant mother of five taking her tribe out in public. Why? Well, for starters, trying to keep an eye on five children in a grocery store should be an Olympic qualifying event, with mothers who survive unscathed taking home the gold. Still, I was doing a decent job that day . . . until about halfway through our shopping excursion.

In the midst of fending off repeated requests for Laffy Taffy and nodding blindly at the plethora of comments that come when you have five children all talking to you at once, I failed to notice that my toddler was wriggling free from her safety belt.

As soon as I noticed, I gave a straightforward command. "Sweetheart," I said quietly. "You can't stand in the grocery cart. Please sit down." (First-time obedience? Check!)

Then without warning, my daughter's beautiful blue eyes blazed like fire. She looked directly into my face and shouted, "No!" And then, just in case I missed it the first time, she screamed even louder, "NOOOOOOOOOOOOO!" (Respect for authority? Uncheck.)

The other children stopped and looked at me. They were as embarrassed as I was. Actually, I take that back. I was far more embarrassed than the four of them combined. I felt my face flush and quickly glanced around. One after another, neighboring shoppers averted their gazes, and several people hastily pushed their carts around the corner. Nobody wanted to be stuck in the aisle with the pregnant mother of five in the middle of a full-blown toddler meltdown.

Nope. I definitely was *not* medaling in the grocery-store Olympics that day. Actually, I take that back too. Because had they given a medal for rapidly rounding up four flustered children and hustling them out of the store while a hysterical toddler is flailing wildly in your arms, I would have taken the gold for sure.

It wasn't the first time we'd made a hasty exodus from a

public place. This toddler wasn't like my other toddlers. If I said it was black, she said it was white. If I said sit, she stood. If I said no, she said yes. As I gathered her in my arms and hurried through the store with my wailing child balanced on my very pregnant belly, it occurred to me how prideful I'd been toward that other Walmart mom.

God used that shopping trip to humble me. Sometimes humility comes in the secret places of our hearts. Other times it happens in the diaper aisle of Walmart. In this case, I can't help but picture God with a little grin on His face as He watched me grappling with my tantrumming toddler.

I was twelve years into my motherhood journey, and I was still just warming up. I was still becoming. The fact that I'd graduated from a parenting class with flying colors didn't make me immune to the process. All it did was fill me with enough false confidence to make me unable to show grace to another mom who, like me, was also on the road to becoming.

Believe me, twenty-six years of motherhood has provided me with plenty of reminders about how much I'm in need of grace myself. Along this motherhood journey, I've come to realize that God's grace is indeed sufficient. And what led me to that conclusion? Time and experience. There's no substitute for them, because they're part of the journey of *becoming*. Sometimes we get it right, and sometimes—well, sometimes we just leave our cart full of groceries in the middle of the aisle and call it a day.

THE MYTH OF QUIET TIME

Becoming the mom God wants you to be takes time, experience, and grace. But it also takes one more thing: intention. Simply put, we become what we purpose to become—what we're intentional about becoming. I call this kind of purposeful living holy. *Holy* means "set apart." When we set ourselves apart from the rest of the world and raise our children in a way that brings honor and glory to God, that's what will be required of us: holy intention. An intention that is set apart from the ordinary view of motherhood.

We become what we purpose to become— what we're intentional about becoming.

If your intention is to raise up a generation of kids who will know the One who created them and walk in right relationship with Him, it needs to start with you! MomStrong moms are intentional about getting to know God's Word, because when we do so, we get to know God Himself. I know that may sound intimidating, but precious mom, it's not as hard to get to know Him as you might think. You may not know it yet, but God honors every bit of time you spend with Him. In fact, I believe He multiplies it. He knows every detail of your life, and He understands—more than anyone else—the season of life you're in.

While I'm a fan of deep, rich studies of the Word, I also know there are seasons that simply don't allow for it. So if you have a tiny one in your arms right now, here's some good news: you don't have to do an inductive Bible study to know God intimately. For young mothers, the season of "all hands on deck" seems to leave little time for that ever-elusive "quiet time." I want to encourage you not to give up—because that's exactly what the enemy wants you to do. I say, "Take that, Satan! We're gonna get into our Bibles anyway!"

When our kids are little, it's easy to feel overwhelmed and alone in our relationship with God. I know. I get it. So for all you sleep-deprived moms, stay with me for just a minute more, because God has been patiently teaching me something while I've been pulling all-nighters times seven. He wants to teach you something too.

Several years ago, after the birth of my sixth child and after *another* all-nighter with a fussy baby, I was out on my deck in the early-morning hours, literally crying out to God as I watched the sun come up over Mount Saint Helens. I felt alone and disconnected because I hadn't been spending time with Him. It wasn't that I didn't want to; it was just that there was literally no time when I wasn't with my kids. And when I wasn't with my kids, I was trying to take a shower by myself. This is the reality for most moms in this season of life—am I right?

That particular morning, I poured out my guilt-ridden heart loud enough for anyone within earshot of our little house to hear: "God! I need Your help! I can't do this by myself!"

And do you know what happened next? God met me right there, with my tearstained face, my cup of decaf, and my Kleenex in hand, and He set me free. In that moment, I understood something about God that I'd missed before, something crucial to the process of becoming more like Him: God is just as present when I'm unloading the dishwasher as He is when I'm doing an inductive Bible study.

Did you catch that? Because it's just as true for you as it

was for me that morning. God isn't bothered by the sounds of children playing at your feet or irritated by the fact that your quiet time bears little to no resemblance to the quiet time you may have had before you became a mother. He knows you're in the process of becoming. After all, it was His design. And He wants to meet you where you are so you can walk with Him to the next leg of your journey.

> *God is just as present when you're unloading the dishwasher as He is when you're doing an inductive Bible study.*

After that, I did what God asked me to do: I invited the kids into my quiet time. I picked up spiral-bound notebooks when they went on sale at the grocery store, and I started reading a children's Bible with my kids. In the years we did this, God taught me as much as (and sometimes more than) He'd taught me in the seasons I devoted to intensive studies. It really was a lesson in how God blesses our efforts to know Him. Just through my reading a simple passage with the kids each morning before school and giving them time to write (or draw) what they were learning about, God blessed me tenfold. I was able to watch my children in their own journeys of becoming more like Jesus as we learned and grew together.

If you're in a season that defies quiet, God understands. He's not looking for fancy—He's asking for faithfulness.

MOM**STRONG** MOM,
FOCUS ON WHO YOU'RE BECOMING

Precious mom, hear me say this loud and clear: God loves you. Becoming the mother He created you to be is worth every ounce of effort you put into it. No matter what season of motherhood you are in, I encourage you to embrace the spiritual discipline of spending time with God, no matter what that time looks like. Trust me, He will honor the effort, whether you're doing an in-depth Bible study or reading a five-minute devotion from a children's Bible with your kids.

God has a special place in His heart for those who are bringing up children. The Bible says, "He gently leads those that have young" (Isaiah 40:11, NIV). The key word here is *gently*. If God is gentle with mothers, we need to be gentle too—both with our fellow becomers and with ourselves.

MomStrong moms never lose sight of the goal of becoming. Even when the days are long and the struggles feel overwhelming, God is hard at work helping you become more like Christ. Be patient, sweet mom. You'll get there.

PRAYER POINTS FOR A
MOM WHO'S BECOMING

- Pray that you will become the mom God wants you to be and that your children will become the people God wants them to be (see Ephesians 4:14-15).

- Pray that God will help you extend grace to other moms in your life (see Matthew 7:1).
- Pray that you will be intentional about setting aside time with God, even if it doesn't look like a traditional quiet time right now (see Psalm 119:16).

Chapter 5

YOUR KIDS DON'T NEED YOU TO DO IT ALL

Kindergarten was an exciting time for me—it was a whole new world of people to meet and twenty-some classmates to discuss my five years of life with. It was also the first time anyone ever said to my parents, "Heidi talks too much." Apparently, though, I didn't get the memo, because by the time first grade rolled around, the notes section of my report card read, "Great attitude; could work on not talking so much." Second grade went along fine, except for that pesky little incident when I wound up in the principal's office for—you guessed it—talking.

By the time I reached high school, I was putting my gift of

gab to better use by interning as a youth leader at our church and teaching a small-group Bible study. Talking may have gotten me into trouble as a kid, but it was also a gift—and something I loved. I didn't know it as a child, of course, but I was born to talk and teach. I was hardwired for a purpose.

And so are you.

Like me, you came into this world with a unique, God-given purpose—one that's written into your DNA. God is going to use your personality, your talents, and your natural inclinations for His glory. Yes, even your grade school report cards. Even the hard things. No—*especially* the hard things.

Not only does God use your natural bent and wiring, He also uses the obstacles you face for His good purposes. The sick child, the rebellious teen, the learning curve you faced when you had your first baby, the heartbreak of loss, the struggle to get in shape and reclaim your identity after giving birth—all of these challenges carry redemptive power with them when they are placed in the hands of your heavenly Father.

Motherhood is just the beginning of God's great adventure for you.

I know it's easy to lose sight of our purpose in the midst of diapers and dishes. In fact, mothers often struggle to find their purpose. But make no mistake: the woman who becomes a mother will be transformed in the process, and in the midst of motherhood, her purpose and calling will be refined and renewed.

Precious mom, if you're struggling to find your purpose, take heart! Motherhood is just the beginning of God's great adventure for you. Through motherhood's many ups and downs, God is providing you with on-the-job training for a lifetime of Kingdom purpose. But first, all moms must go through a season of surrender.

THE PEANUT-BUTTER-AND-JELLY SEASON

Several years ago, when I was speaking at an event in New York, I met a mom who tearfully confessed that although she was trying her best to "look the part" of a happy mom of little ones, on the inside she was bitter. She missed her freedom. No more quick trips to her favorite coffee shop. No more prestigious career. Gone were the days of a neat and tidy house. Life as a stay-at-home mom was not what she'd expected.

Part of her felt blindsided by the transition. When she made the decision to stay home with her kids, she hadn't envisioned the toll it might take on her emotionally. Her husband's life seemed to be going on just as it always had, but she felt like she had stalled out. Hearing about her husband's power lunches and promotions at work only deepened her frustration. Where was *her* promotion? Where was the recognition of the work *she* was doing?

I leaned in and hugged my new friend. I understood. The transition from "me" to "us" can be a bumpy one. We talked for a few minutes more before her deeper hurt—the real hurt—bubbled to the surface.

"I'm just a mom!" she said softly. "I used to be someone. Now I spend my days covered in peanut butter and jelly! I don't even know who I am anymore."

I asked the Lord for His wisdom. As she continued to share her frustrations, it became clear to me that this discouraged mom didn't need the do over she was searching for; she needed a dream to match the season of life she was in. She also needed a hug and a reminder that God did have a purpose for her—even in the peanut-butter-and-jelly season of motherhood.

You need a dream to match the season of life you're in.

Truth be told, the concept of seasonal living isn't very popular with this generation. Somewhere along the line, someone sold us the myth that moms can do it all and have it all. Every time we go through the checkout at the grocery store, we see pictures on the covers of magazines of moms who have the whole package: money, healthy marriages, material possessions, and dream careers. In pursuit of this illusive dream, many moms today are pushing the peanut-butter-and-jelly season aside in an attempt to "just get through it." In reality, however, this season serves a precious purpose: not only is it formative in the lives of our children, but it also teaches us the beauty of surrender.

Jesus knew all about surrender: "Not my will, but yours be done" (Luke 22:42, NIV). His example resonates in my mother-heart as I think of the many times He has asked me to surrender my plans for His. But Jesus will never ask us to do anything He hasn't already done more fully and more painfully than we ever will.

There was a season when I had to stop doing almost everything I wanted to do simply because the needs of our children were more pressing. And so, rather than say yes to every opportunity, I began instead to say a gentle no.

- "No, I can't lead the Bible study this fall. Thank you for asking me."
- "No, I can't join you at the beach for the women's retreat. Thank you so much for inviting me."
- "No, that's the baby's naptime."
- "No, I am homeschooling from nine to two. Can we do a Saturday morning instead?"
- "No, I would love to come speak, but our sixth baby is due around that time."

Those noes were my surrender.

As I look back, I realize these weren't just simple answers. They were a beautiful exchange. In surrendering lunch dates, book groups, and coffee runs for nap schedules, homemaking, and homeschooling, I said a resounding *yes* to investing my whole heart into motherhood. And in that surrender, I found new purpose. And in that new purpose, I found joy.

I want to be clear: it's not easy to surrender to the season of young children. Mine was definitely a peanut-butter-and-jelly type of surrender, full of sticky places and moments of frustration and struggle. And yet I wouldn't trade it for the world, because now I have the gift of perspective.

Not long ago my husband and I were sitting by our fireplace when he touched my knee. "Take note, Heidi," he said with a gentleness in his voice that made me look up from my laptop.

"This might be the last time we will see our four younger children acting like . . . *children*."

I stopped writing and watched our kids for a few minutes. Our fifteen-year-old son was playing some sort of chasing game with his six-year-old sister. She squealed as he scooped her up and threatened to drop her into the "hot lava" that covered the dining room floor in its entirety.

Twenty years ago, I might not have stopped to soak it in. I soak it in now, because I realize that one day I'll miss all the activity and noise. One day the season of hot-lava squeals will be over with these four, as it is with my older three. Perspective changes things.

That doesn't mean surrender will be easy, but it helps to remember that this season isn't going to last forever.

If you're struggling to come to terms with your own surrender, allow me to encourage you a bit. Part of becoming MomStrong means you may have to give up the good in order to gain something better. Every mom has a different barometer for what surrendering is, but—trust me—when you feel the pains of surrender, they're really just birth pains. You're going to get something far better than what you're surrendering. You're raising lifelong friends and confidants. The memories of watching your children become who God has made them to be is worth a lifetime of surrender.

Easy for me to say? My surrender was found in the throes of being a mom to seven independent children—in sleepless nights and sticky dinner tables. I suppose you could argue that what I gave up—my career as a receptionist and part-time Tupperware consultant—wasn't much in terms of money or prestige. But try this one on for size: on November 24, 2015,

Elisabeth Hasselbeck, a successful cohost at Fox News, shocked her audience when she announced she was leaving her lucrative job in order to focus on her children. "I am taking a new position as CBO—chief breakfast officer—at our house with the kids, and that does mean that in about a month, I'll be leaving my Fox News family," she said during the morning broadcast, adding that being at home with her children in the mornings is her new priority. "I'm in a season where the kids need the best of me, not the rest of me."[1]

Your greatest accomplishment as a mom may not be something you do but someone you raise.

Hasselbeck was making an exchange. She was trading something good for something better. She was acknowledging that the season for impacting children goes by quickly and that she didn't want to miss it. That's not to say that moms can't work outside the home—it's true that many moms (myself included) work to help support their families. The point is that we need to surrender ourselves to what God wants us to do. We need to be willing to do what He says is best, not what our flesh wants or what the world says we should do.

I heard it said that my greatest accomplishment as a mom may not be something I do—but someone I raise. And I believe it. That's worth a season of surrender.

A DREAM FOR THIS SEASON

I get it. When you're eyebrow deep in peanut butter and jelly, it's hard to see beyond naptime, let alone years into the future. But that's *exactly* what we need to do.

MomStrong moms don't surrender their dreams. They ask God to give them *His* dreams. They believe that as they walk out this life, God will walk with them. And as He does, He'll plant seeds for new dreams along the way—dreams that are equal to the season they're in. Why do I believe this? Because I trust the promises of God. Jeremiah 29:11 says, "'I know the plans I have for you,' says the Lord. 'They are plans for good and not for disaster, to give you a future and a hope.'" Instead of wishing away the sticky surrender years, moms who believe they were born for a purpose can fully surrender to the seasons of motherhood. What makes this kind of countercultural surrender possible? Faith. These moms know that God is doing something beyond what they can see right now.

You have been divinely placed right where you are for a reason.

Precious mom, your life is of unimaginable worth to God. You are not an accident. You have been divinely placed right where you are for a reason. It may not sound very divine when you're surrounded by laundry, dishes, and diapers, but be encouraged. God has placed you right where He needs you to be. Letting this simple truth sink into your heart is a game changer.

So the next time you're tempted to doubt the significance of your role in God's great story, remember who made you. The enemy wants you to believe that your role is insignificant, but don't buy it. Satan lies to you about your worth because he's worried you're going to emerge from the sweet act of surrender stronger than you ever dared to believe.

God uses every season of motherhood to make us into women He can use for His divine purpose. So lean in to the season God has you in, sweet mama. Surrender yourself to His plan. Ask the Lord to show you what He wants you to learn in this season—and expect Him to give you exactly the grace you need to experience joy in the midst of it. After all, surrendering to life's seasonal rhythms is all about grace—grace for the season we're in and grace for the seasons to come.

THE PASSION PRINCIPLE

I used to laugh when people asked me what my hobbies were. When I had six young children at home, I figured the blank look in my eyes said it all. *I mean, come on—I'm a mom!* Most years, I was pretty easy to please: I enjoyed silence and unaccompanied trips to the bathroom. And honestly? I rarely got either of those things.

For a few years, my passion became my Crock-Pot. I was consumed with figuring out how to feed our tribe on a pastor's salary. I scoured cookbooks for recipes I could use over and over, and eventually I got it down . . . just in time to figure out how to homeschool our kids. The sheer demands of my growing young family left little time for me to pursue anything else.

Eventually, when the little ones no longer required so much of my time, I began to get back to things I'd naturally gravitated toward before having children. For instance, I love to speak. I thrive on communicating to other people what God is teaching me. But since my opportunities to speak were limited by my choice to homeschool our children, I took up blogging as another way to use that gift.

I know a lot of folks who can't stand putting pen to paper (my husband is one of them), but for me, writing turned out to be an outlet. It was something that both energized and relaxed me. When my other friends were scrapbooking, I was figuring out how to keep an online journal. Finding just the right words to express my rawest emotions became a passion for me, even if I had only a moment here and there to do it.

Looking back, I realize that my kindergarten teacher's quarterly report card notes were really windows into what would become part of God's unique purpose for my life. When I'm teaching or speaking, I can almost feel the warmth of God's smile. As the Olympic runner Eric Liddell says in the movie *Chariots of Fire*, when I do the things I was made to do, "I feel [God's] pleasure."

Statistically speaking, there's a good chance you don't love speaking as much as I do. But I have a hunch that there's *something* you love. Other people may have already noticed a special gift in you. If you're not sure what that is, take some time to ask yourself a few questions:

- What am I good at?
- What activities or tasks energize me?
- What do I like to do in my free time?
- What could I teach someone else to do?
- Where are my efforts most fruitful?

In other words, what do you do naturally and with the most ease? If you take time to notice what you lean toward doing in your spare time (or what you would do if you actually had spare time), you're probably close to discovering what God has gifted you to do—what your passion is. If you can identify your passion, chances are, your purpose isn't far behind!

So what happens when you have a passion but you're in the middle of the most time-intensive years of mothering? It's time to repurpose your passion! Repurposing passion allows you to make the most of whatever season you're in and use your gifts and abilities to bless your family. I like to encourage moms to direct their God-given passion toward their family during the little-kid years. For me, that meant diving headlong into Jay's passion. I was still using the gifts and skills God had given me; it's just that I was doing it in a context that helped build our family's identity, and in doing so, I was also setting a trajectory for years to come.

My husband was a pastor for nearly twenty years, and because Jay's role included opening our home to others hundreds of times during the years, I learned to develop the gift of hospitality. I hosted worship team practices and meetings at our home, which allowed me to remain an active part of what Jay was doing while at the same time being with the kids.

Church ministry is especially busy during the Christmas and Easter seasons, so as much as I wanted to be part of the choir or outreach groups, it simply wasn't realistic for me with so many little ones. Instead, I organized a team to serve dessert at the Christmas musicals my husband was producing. It was my way of using my gifts in harmony with the season of life my family was in. Focusing my passion toward my family and our ministry helped guide the trajectory of our mission as a family and set the tone for the way our family would do life together.

MomStrong moms know that repurposed passion is just another way of saying surrendered passion—trading something good for something better. When we repurpose our passions to fit the season of life we're in, amazing things happen. Joy happens. Growth happens. We're invited to watch as God takes what we offer Him and uses it for the Kingdom. After all, God's purposes and passion for His people are always in season.

If you aren't sure how to incorporate your passions into this particular season of motherhood, just ask the Lord. I promise, He's waiting to show you.

LIFE AFTER LITTLE ONES

On our twenty-fifth wedding anniversary, my husband informed me that we'd had a toddler in our home for twenty-two years in a row. We had our first child in 1991. When this book goes to print, our youngest child will be six. It's no wonder I like chocolate in my peanut butter ice cream. Twenty-four years of chasing after a toddler will do that to you!

When I watched my first grandchild enter into the world, the truth of this divine call of motherhood took on new meaning. That's when I realized that I'd spent the past twenty-three years raising the mother of my grandchildren! No wonder the enemy is so consumed with taking down families. Your investment is not only influencing your children's lives; it's also shaping the lives of your grandchildren, your great-grandchildren, and beyond!

Through motherhood, you are impacting the world for good, one young life at a time. But full-time motherhood lasts only as long as you have dependent children in your home. For some of us, that season is an extended one. Maybe, like me, you'll have a toddler in your home for twenty-some years. Or maybe you'll graduate your only child from high school after eighteen years, and then a new season will begin.

Through motherhood, you are impacting the world for good, one young life at a time.

While you'll always be a mother, your active role in mothering will draw to a close sooner than you can possibly imagine. MomStrong moms prepare for this season before it arrives. Just as we want to be ready at the start of our motherhood journey, we also want to be ready as it draws to a close. It may be hard to imagine a time when you won't be changing diapers, coordinating car pools, or homeschooling, but believe me, you won't always be mothering little ones or making sure your teen studies for that exam.

When I was in the middle of toddler taming, it never occurred to me that my full-time mothering gig would come to an end one day. But over the years I've seen hundreds of women experience the empty-nest syndrome. And let me tell you, this transition is rarely as graceful as it sounds in magazines or mommy blogs. When motherhood is a part of your identity, watching the last child wave good-bye and take off down the driveway is no small thing. It takes a strong mother to slip gracefully into the next season of life.

MomStrong moms don't fear the empty nest. They see it as a new season, full of new dreams and opportunities. This is when mentors (those "older women" referred to in Titus 2:3-5) are especially important. They give us perspective and help us even out the rough places of motherhood.

I heard this illustrated beautifully several years ago at a conference where my friend Steve Lambert was speaking. He spoke about his wonderful wife, Jane, and her season of transitioning out of full-time motherhood. My ears perked up. This man loved his wife! Instead of waiting for the empty-nest season to simply arrive for his wife, Steve decided to be proactive. When their youngest child was still in high school, he began to encourage Jane to pursue her passions:

> As my wife Jane's days of active motherhood began to wind down in the 1990s, I encouraged her to begin looking at the next season of her life. What did the Lord have for her to do next? What gifts did she have that could bless others? How could she continue to bring forth God's Kingdom in the midst of a broken world? In her case, she took what she had learned as a homeschool mother and wrote an award-winning, bestselling curriculum that's been used by more than a hundred thousand families in the past twenty years. Five in a Row is an extension of Jane's mothering ministry, and it has changed the lives of more than five hundred thousand other children over the years.[2]

Jane found a place for her passion through writing, but for you, it might be teaching art, volunteering as a museum docent, working with hospice, or doing lay chaplaincy at a nearby hospital. It might be cooking and serving in a homeless shelter or even mentoring young mothers as they begin their journeys. Whatever it is, do it with all your heart and soul! Your passions are part of God's plan, and He wants to use them both now and in the next season of your life.

MOM**STRONG** MOM, FIND YOUR PASSION

What is your passion? Perhaps your calling for the next season will include going back and finishing nursing school or getting a degree in education. Or maybe you'll learn a foreign language and volunteer on a short-term mission trip. The world is filled with possibilities, and even before the season of full-time mothering draws to a close, it's wise to prayerfully figure out what the world needs and how you can help fill that need with the gifts and experiences the Lord has given you.

In the meantime, keep stoking the fires of the unique gifts God has given specifically to you, because He wants to use these irreplaceable years of child raising to equip you for what lies beyond. Take your God-given talent and set it apart for God's use. The Lord will give you the strength to discover His purpose and then walk in it, if you ask Him.

And remember, becoming MomStrong isn't just about raising strong, confident, godly kids. It's also about discovering what God has set in His heart for you to do with the time you've been given—no matter what season you're in.

PRAYER POINTS FOR A
PURPOSEFUL MOM

- Pray that your children will develop their gifts and talents and sense God's pleasure as they do (see 1 Corinthians 12:4-6).
- Pray that God will show you how you can repurpose your passion for the current season of life you're in (see 1 Timothy 6:12).
- Pray that God will start preparing you for the calling He has for you when your nest is empty (see Isaiah 43:19).

Chapter 6

WHEN YOUR PLANS GET TURNED UPSIDE DOWN

"*Do* you trust Me?"

This was the question I heard the Lord speaking to my heart as I drove along the Oregon coast, en route to a meeting with my agent about the book you're holding in your hands. My alarm had woken me at 6:00 a.m., giving me just enough time to make the ninety-minute drive, meet my agent over breakfast, and drive back in time for a staff meeting at the camp where Jay and I were serving for a week.

It was a cold, damp October morning as I headed south on Highway 101. About twenty minutes into the drive, my 2003 Suburban began to overheat. I stopped at a gas station in the middle of nowhere and stood looking at the car. I had no idea what to do. I tried to call Jay, but the phone reception was so poor back at camp that I couldn't get through. So I did the next best thing—I phoned our friends in Kansas City.

"You're up early, kid!" Steve chided me.

I wasn't in a mood for joking around.

"Hi. Yeah. I'm out here in the middle of nowhere in Oregon, and I think the car is overheating. Can you help me?"

Steve patiently talked me through how to take off the radiator cap while I lugged what I *thought* was the water hose from the pay-per-use station to the car. I'll digress a little from the story here to mention that it was actually the air hose. Yep. I did that. Smack-dab in front of a carload of very amused (and, I might add, rather unchivalrous) Oregon fishermen, I put air in the radiator instead of water.

The noise from the air hose was ridiculously loud, but since Steve wasn't there to see what I was doing (and since *I* clearly had no idea what I was doing), I didn't realize that it shouldn't have made any noise at all. Ignorant but determined, I tried again. More noise.

Man, did I wish my husband was there.

By the time I finally figured out what I'd done, my face was red from embarrassment and my clothes were filthy. And I was screaming mad at all those guys who'd just sat there without offering to help. I was a mess, really. And for more reasons than I realized at the moment.

I finally got some actual water in my car, and Steve stayed on the line long enough to make sure the car temperature returned to normal before I headed farther south, where cell service was even iffier and gas stations were even more scarce. As I headed toward Lincoln City, wave after wave of anxiety swept over me. *What if the car breaks down again? What then?* From there, my thoughts spiraled out of control. *What am I even doing out here in the middle of nowhere? Who do I think I am, writing a book? What do I have to offer mothers?*

The breakdown of my car had triggered a whole flood of other insecurities. Suddenly I was not a confident wife and mother. I was who the enemy said I was: Anxiety Girl.

Taking advantage of the fact that I was alone (i.e., sans children) in my car, I started talking out loud to God. At first it was just a simple prayer, but before long my prayers became tears. I was struggling. Finances were tight—really tight. Jay and I had taken a huge leap of faith when we decided to follow God's call on my life to write and speak more, and deep down I doubted whether we would have enough money to make it through the next few months, let alone the next year. I'd undergone emergency surgery two months earlier, and our changes in employment had put us at the mercy of a new national health care system. The hospital bills were piling up. On top of that, another child was getting ready to move out, rocking the family dynamic and causing stress and a little sadness, too.

My mind was swimming with questions. If God wanted me to do this, why weren't things just falling into place? Why was it such a struggle? Why did I feel so inadequate? Why would God give me seven beautiful children and then call me to spend time away from them writing and speaking? The guilt was overwhelming.

Here's what I didn't realize at the time: this entire conversation I was having "with God" was really a fight between me and the enemy of my soul. I was allowing the voice of condemnation to drown out that still, small voice of conviction.

The voice of conviction lifts us up and sets our feet back on the Rock. But unless we listen for that voice, condemnation creeps in, turning us into the victim. In order to tune in to the truth, we have to be still. And at that moment, I was not still.

"God!" I cried. "Where are you? Are you listening? Answer me!"

Silence. The sun was coming up. I blinked away hot tears as I rounded the last corner into Lincoln City. I was almost there when I heard my answer—a still, small voice that couldn't be denied. *How can you say I'll supply all your needs if you've never truly trusted Me with a real need in your life? How can you write about My sustaining grace and provision if you can't even bear witness to it?*

I was beginning to understand. While I fully believed in God, I realized that, at my core, I was a control freak. I wanted guarantees. I wanted God to work out *my* plan, not *His*. But the guarantee that God's plan will work out for good isn't simply temporary; it's eternal. His plans are always best, but they are rarely as straightforward or predictable as what we would plan ourselves.

God asks us to do things by faith. He wants us to trust Him, no matter what circumstances we find ourselves in. Nothing more, nothing less. The journey we are on is designed to help us trust God in ways we don't expect and can't foresee. I began to see that if I was going to write *Becoming MomStrong* from a place of authenticity, I needed to trust that God would use me—along with all my fears, failures, and insecurities—for His glory. My story, His glory.

I eventually made it to my meeting, and in the days that

followed, I determined to listen more carefully for God's assurance. I determined to take everything—even the things that felt inconsequential—before the Lord in prayer. When doubts crept in, when I felt anything but MomStrong, I knew that the battle for my mind and emotions was real. I could feel the inner struggle to surrender and bear witness to God's redeeming work in my life, to believe that He knows what He is doing. As I confessed my fears and asked God to replace them with faith, He did.

The journey we are on is designed to help us trust God in ways we don't expect and can't foresee.

The choice to cry out to Him is always ours to make. The question we usually find ourselves asking afterward is *Why did I wait so long?* He is always a whisper away. You see, when we refuse to listen to the enemy's voice of condemnation, our struggles become the very catalyst to strengthen our faith. James says that's what struggles are for: "Dear brothers and sisters, when troubles of any kind come your way, consider it an opportunity for great joy" (James 1:2).

Precious mom, what trial are you facing right now? Whatever it is, I encourage you to listen for that still, small voice and trust in the conviction of God. And when you're traveling alone in a remote area in a "gently used" vehicle, take an extra bottle of water along—just in case. You're welcome.

THE HIDDEN GIFT OF TRIALS

Have you ever noticed how many of the psalms were written during times of difficulty?

> Though a mighty army surrounds me,
> my heart will not be afraid.
> Even if I am attacked,
> I will remain confident.
>
> PSALM 27:3

> This I declare about the LORD:
> He alone is my refuge, my place of safety;
> he is my God, and I trust him.
>
> PSALM 91:2

> The LORD is my light and my salvation—
> so why should I be afraid?
> The LORD is my fortress, protecting me from danger,
> so why should I tremble?
>
> PSALM 27:1

If we read between the lines of these psalms, we get the distinct impression that the psalmist is facing some pretty serious challenges: being surrounded by an army, needing a place of refuge, facing danger and fear and anxiety. Maybe we're not facing a literal army, but my guess is that most of us have felt like we're in a battle at some point or at the very least in need of a place of rest and protection.

Likewise, many of the New Testament epistles were written from prisons. Some of the most powerful sections of Scripture were written by authors who found themselves in circumstances beyond their control—circumstances they never would have chosen themselves. Paul wrote the book of Philippians when he was in the custody of the Roman government, yet he still clung to the promise of God's faithfulness: "This same God who takes care of me will supply all your needs from his glorious riches, which have been given to us in Christ Jesus" (Philippians 4:19).

In the same way that fear can test our trust, trials can also test our trust. Let me say that again, because I need to hear it too: trials test our trust.

In her song "Hard Times," Amy Grant writes,

Hard times come
And they'll come till we're done.

You know what? She's right. Hard times come—but they're not here to torture us; they're here to teach us. We either learn from them or we don't.

One of the mistakes we often make as mothers is thinking that our children should never see us get upset or wrestle through something. This is simply not true (not to mention impossible). Struggle is a part of life. The question isn't whether our children should see our struggles and burdens. The question is, Does our response to trials point our children to Jesus Christ even as we stumble and struggle along the way?

If we tell our children that we trust God, but we're living in a constant state of panic and distrust, what are we saying with our lives? Through our actions, we put our trust in God on display for our children. Our responses to the pressures of this world are shaping an entire generation. The way we handle failure, financial difficulty, loss, and pain speaks volumes about what we really believe.

If we tell our children that we trust God, but we're living in a constant state of panic and distrust, what are we saying with our lives?

In Psalm 20:7, David says, "Some trust in chariots and some in horses, but we trust in the name of the LORD our God" (NIV). Allow me to put that into contemporary mom-speak for you: "Some trust in financial stability, some trust in homeschooling, some trust in medicine, some trust in [fill in your own blank], but I choose to trust in the name of the Lord!"

There are so many things that seem easier to trust than the Lord—after all, He is invisible. We like to *see* what we're putting our trust in. But isn't it part of faith to trust our future to a God we can't see? The truth is, anything other than Jesus will eventually let us down. In Psalm 28:7-8, David says: "The LORD is my strength and shield. I trust him with all my heart. He helps me, and my heart is filled with joy. I burst out in songs of thanksgiving. The LORD gives his people strength. He is a safe fortress for his anointed king."

Is the Lord your strength and shield? Take a moment to check your heart. It's easy to operate in the world and forget that God is our true source of protection and power.

Look at the list below and ask yourself, *Who am I trusting for these things?*

- finances
- wisdom
- peace
- security
- strength
- healing

Does your life demonstrate a trust in God's provision? In His goodness? In His Word? In His timing? It's critical that it does. Why? Because we can't give our kids what we don't have. If we don't put our trust in the Lord, how can we expect them to?

Are you struggling? Look up! Don't be overcome by fear or anxiety. Remember that God can use these hard times to teach us and to put our trust to the test.

WHOM DO WE TRUST (REALLY)?

Mothers carry so much responsibility. After all, we're the gate-keepers of the next generation, and the next generation is up against a fierce war. Even in the last few years, I've seen the culture change rapidly. Like never before, Christians today are being asked to show where their trust really lies. What's more, we're being asked to live it out.

Here are just a few battlefields where the war is raging:

- The Supreme Court has redefined marriage. *Whom do you trust?*

- Displays of the Ten Commandments have been removed from many public places, even as satanists attempt to erect a pagan statue in cities like Detroit.[1] *Whom do you trust?*
- A football coach from Bremerton, Washington, came under investigation for simply praying at the fifty-yard line where his team could see him.[2] *Whom do you trust?*
- The culture says your children can choose their gender. *Whom do you trust?*

We'll never be able to release our children to God's loving plan for them unless we accept that He is big enough, wise enough, and good enough to be trusted. Our trust in God is being put to the test every day—and if you weren't sure of that before, all you need to do is glance at the news for proof.

God is big enough, wise enough, and good enough to be trusted.

I'm a bit of a newshound. My grandparents were also avid newsies, following local, national, and world events via television and newspaper on a daily basis. They were fierce, my grandparents. Living through the Great Depression and losing several members of your family to illnesses like smallpox and German measles will do that to you. Yet I never once heard my grandparents question whether God could be trusted.

It's harder to be a newshound these days. First of all, there's a whole lot more news available out there than any one person can possibly take in. At my last count, there were more than a dozen ways to get the news at any given moment. Yet for all that access, we're no better off than we were when my grandparents had just one newspaper to turn to. In fact, I'd say all this un-fettered access has made things harder, not easier.

News of ISIS, a struggling economy, and a culture sliding further away from God can make a strong heart feel faint. We can easily forget that God is still on His throne. Before we know it, the "what if" monster creeps up while we're not looking, and pretty soon, we're not trusting anymore. We're afraid.

I'll never forget seeing my grandmother after a heart attack nearly took her life. Tubes covered her entire body, and oxygen was being delivered to her by even more tubes. The only sounds in the room were the hushed tones of the ventilator. In. Out. In. Out.

Days passed. When Grandmother was finally able to talk, I couldn't hold back my tears. "I thought you were going to die!" I cried.

Grandmother's soft reply came in rhythm with the machines. "Heidi, has God ever failed you?"

Sure! I thought. *He failed me when you had a heart attack!*

But Grandmother was wise. She'd learned to trust God. "God's purpose is good," she said to me. "Don't doubt Him just because you're afraid. When God takes me home, it will be because He knows that's what's best."

As usual, she was right. My fear was causing me to doubt God's goodness and sovereignty.

Maybe you're afraid too. Maybe your struggle to allow God's

plan to unfold in your life and the lives of your children is harder than you imagined it would be. Maybe, like me, you need to trust God even though you thought your plan just might have been better.

We do that, don't we? We second-guess the One who knows us best, the One whose plans for us are to prosper us and not to harm us (see Jeremiah 29:11). Oh, precious mom, your hope will never be found in our government or in a husband or even in yourself. But any confidence you put in the Creator is well placed.

Our hope is never going to be found in our government or in a husband or even in ourselves. It's only found in God.

One of the reasons I love the Psalms so much is that David is so transparent in his human attempt to walk with his Creator. The source of his confidence and stability wasn't his own strength but God. And yet he struggled. This man who referred to himself as the apple of God's eye (see Psalm 17:8, NIV) struggled with fear. One minute he was praising God, and the next he was crying out for rescue—just like the rest of us!

When you find yourself struggling as David did, ask yourself, "Has God ever failed me?" The answer is a clear and resounding no. Even if it seems like He is absent. Even when we make mistakes and choose to walk in disobedience, God says He uses *all things* for good. He is in control—even when we feel out of control—which means we can quiet our hearts and rest, knowing that God will never let us go.

When we realize that God sees our frailty and understands our worry, it's easier to see His heart for us. God loves us, even in our times of doubt and unbelief. As the song goes, "The times they are a-changin'." But God doesn't change. He remains the same: "Jesus Christ is the same yesterday, today, and forever" (Hebrews 13:8). Even when my plans fail, His never will.

HELP MY UNBELIEF!

I love Robert Robinson's hymn "Come Thou Fount of Every Blessing" because I can so easily see myself reflected in its words:

> *Prone to wander, Lord, I feel it,*
> *Prone to leave the God I love;*
> *Here's my heart, O take and seal it;*
> *Seal it for thy courts above.*

Like Mr. Robinson, I am very aware of my tendency to wander away from the protection of my heavenly Father. We all struggle with periods of unbelief, but thank God—He understands our weaknesses and promises to strengthen us through the Bible and the indwelling peace of the Holy Spirit, our Comforter.

Perhaps the most difficult time to believe that God has a good plan is when our children are suffering. Notice the interaction Jesus had with the father of a boy who was afflicted by an evil spirit:

"The spirit often throws him into the fire or into water, trying to kill him. Have mercy on us and help us, if you can."

"What do you mean, 'If I can'?" Jesus asked. "Anything is possible if a person believes."

The father instantly cried out, "I do believe, but help me overcome my unbelief!"

MARK 9:22-24

I love the raw honesty of this father before the Master. He laid down his pride and blurted it out: "I want to trust You, but I'm struggling!" Notice the love of God on full display through His Son. Jesus didn't point a finger at the man or accuse him—He just healed the boy. It had always been in His heart to do so.

Search the Scriptures, and you'll see God's heart for you and for your children.

If you struggle with unbelief, if you wonder if it's safe to leave your children's struggles (and your own) in His hands, it's all right. God understands. He knows we're made of dust. We need only search the Scriptures to see God's heart for us and for our children. Over and over, we see His promises, written for our benefit:

All who listen to me will live in peace,
   untroubled by fear of harm.

PROVERBS 1:33

Despite all these things, overwhelming victory is ours through Christ, who loved us. And I am convinced that nothing can ever separate us from God's love. Neither death nor life, neither angels nor demons, neither our fears for today nor our worries about tomorrow—not even the powers of hell can separate us from God's love. No power in the sky above or in the earth below— indeed, nothing in all creation will ever be able to separate us from the love of God that is revealed in Christ Jesus our Lord.   ROMANS 8:37-39

If you're struggling to believe in God's good plans for you and your family today, God understands. It's in His heart to

- show you a good plan for your life (see Psalm 16:11),
- give you rest (see Matthew 11:28-29),
- replace your weakness with His strength (see Isaiah 40:29),
- declare victory in your life (see 1 Corinthians 15:57), and
- give you peace (John 14:27).

Trust me. Better yet, trust Him! He'll meet you right where you are.

CHOOSING TO TRUST

Every season of motherhood offers new challenges and new chances for us to grow our trust in God. When our children first come to us, our prayers are often for strength—strength to stay up one more night with a sick child. Strength for the toddler-taming years. Strength to meet the physical demands of having little ones at your feet while juggling the responsibilities of a home and a marriage.

It's tempting to believe we're in control when our kids are little. After all, we set the schedule, right? As our children grow, we still need to trust God, but the tone of our prayers changes. Things feel a little less under control (because they are!), and we need wisdom. We need to trust that God will give us the right combination of grace and discipline to get to the root of heart issues rather than just concentrating on external behaviors.

In the teen years and beyond, the season changes yet again. There are new challenges, new fears, and new opportunities to release our children so they can pursue God's amazing plans for them. And we have even less control. I've poured out my heart to God many times as my children have stood at the precipice of adulthood because I realize even more acutely that the trajectory-setting decisions they're making now are theirs alone.

In many ways, the teen years are the final stage of the parenting process. You go from clay (so to speak) to kiln, where the clay is set and ready to be baked and glazed. No wonder so many mothers of teens have that "glazed" look in their eyes!

It's humbling to realize that your years of greatest influence and physical presence are coming to an end. But exciting years lie ahead, because the power of your prayers is just starting to be realized! When mothers begin the season of launching their arrows into the world, an entirely new kind of trust is required: trust that God hears and answers our prayers.

During this season, there are a few areas that are totally in your control. You get to choose to be surrendered to God. You get to choose to spend time in His Word. You get to choose to pray for your children. God's love for His children is fierce. It's tenacious. It's powerful. It's real. And when you pray for your children, heaven is moved into action.

Precious mom, did you know that there's power in your prayers? There is! God says that when we bring our problems, sorrows, fears, and burdens to Him, He promises to help us pray with power: "The Holy Spirit helps us in our weakness. For example, we don't know what God wants us to pray for. But the Holy Spirit prays for us with groanings that cannot be expressed in words" (Romans 8:26).

Did you catch that? The Holy Spirit prays for us. Now that's something every mom needs—the Holy Spirit Himself going to God on her behalf. God is literally saying that the Holy Spirit will pray for us when we are weak. Whether you're struggling with unbelief, doubt, fear, or sickness, His promise is the same. God wants to meet you right where you are. The key is to spend time with Him and learn to live in His presence. That's when we experience His peace.

When it's all said and done, a MomStrong mom doesn't trust in her own abilities; she trusts in a strong, sovereign God.

And in case you find your car overheating on a lonely road, a membership with AAA doesn't hurt either.

MOM**STRONG** MOM, TRUST THE LORD'S PLAN

Precious mom, I know how hard it is to trust the Lord's plan when it unfolds so differently from the agenda you've so carefully mapped out. But in God's hands, the trials that threaten to bring us down are the very things that can build our trust in Him.

You don't have to be perfect in this journey of faith; you just have to be honest. So join me in crying out to the Lord, "I do believe, but help me overcome my unbelief!" The stakes are high—for yourself and for your children.

When was the last time your children saw you on your knees before the Lord? Do they know from the way you live your life that God is trustworthy? Do they see you trusting God? Becoming MomStrong means that we learn to let go of the wheel because we would rather have God be in control than our imperfect selves.

PRAYER POINTS FOR A
MOM WHO TRUSTS GOD'S PLAN

- Pray that the trials you're facing will deepen your trust in the Lord (see 1 Peter 1:6-7).
- Pray that you'll let go of anything you are trusting more than God (see Proverbs 3:5-6).
- Pray that you will be able to release your children to the Lord's plans for them, knowing that He is strong and sovereign (see Proverbs 16:9).

Chapter 7

DON'T GIVE UP!

In 1990, six months after I was married, I began having what I thought were heart problems. I was experiencing episodes of shallow breathing accompanied by a rapid heartbeat for no reason that was obvious to me. I could be taking a shower or making spaghetti—it didn't matter. Without warning, my body would release huge amounts of adrenaline, and I was left a shaking, sweaty-palmed mess. In the months that followed, the attacks became more severe. They kept me up at night and robbed me of peace in broad daylight. I thought I was losing my mind.

It was true that I was having heart problems—but not the kind I thought. As it turned out, I was having the first of what would be many anxiety attacks in the years ahead. My husband was treading in unfamiliar waters with his new wife. As hard as he tried, he couldn't comprehend what I was going through. How could he, when I couldn't comprehend it myself?

After several months of living in abject fear over, well, *nothing*, I finally confided in my doctor. A twenty-minute conversation introduced me to words I had previously reserved for "crazy people," such as *panic attack*. In the end, I was diagnosed with GAD, or generalized anxiety disorder. Great. Twenty years old, and I had a disorder. (And this was *before* kids.)

With mind-numbing accuracy, the doctor explained my symptoms to me as they related to GAD. I sat quietly on the exam table in my thin paper gown. "I see this all the time," he said. "Here's a prescription for Xanax." Before he left, he looked at me squarely and said, "I'm sorry, but I believe you aren't being honest about your life. Most patients with GAD eventually realize that the attacks are not random. You might want to consider counseling. You have all the signs of PTSD." (If you have not had the pleasure of meeting with a psychiatrist, that's "post-traumatic stress disorder.")

And there it was. My first foray into the world of anxiety medications. In the twenty years that followed, I would be on them more than I was off. And very few people knew. After all, I had survived this long without exposing our painful family secret. Domestic violence and Christianity involve an odd mixture of pain and secrecy. Even my grandparents, whom I loved deeply, told me in no uncertain terms to never tell anyone about our private pain, lest it tarnish our reputation in the community. And so, being the good Christian girl that I was, I kept quiet about my panic attacks. I didn't want anyone to think I couldn't "let go and let God," if you know what I mean.

Still, my doctor's diagnosis confirmed that I was in trouble. So I took the counseling route and went to see a pastor in my community. He listened patiently and then, after forty-five minutes, rendered his verdict: "You're angry," he said. "You need to forgive and forget."

Forgive and forget. I couldn't believe it, but that's exactly what he said to me when I went to him, scared and wounded, and dared to tell the truth about my life. They're easy words to say to a person in pain—and unwise ones, as well.

I wasn't buying it.

I was familiar with the forgive-and-forget model. The trouble was, I didn't know anyone who had ever done it successfully. My parents' generation and their parents before them lived by a creed of unspoken pain. I lived by it too. My father hated my grandparents with a peculiar kind of hatred. It practically oozed out of him. My parents hated each other. My siblings hated the fighting—and I hated it all. As far back as I could remember, my life had been filled with strife. I had never seen anyone forgive anyone . . . ever! And forget? You've *got* to be kidding. How could I just sweep away so many layers of pain?

Besides, how do you forgive someone who doesn't want to be forgiven? How do you forgive a person who doesn't even care that they broke you in a thousand different ways? How do you forgive the person who abused you? Is that even possible?

Angry? Mister, you have no idea. Try walking a mile in my shoes, and then tell me to "forgive and forget"!

So there I was. Just past twenty years old. Angry, unforgiving, and afraid. I was operating out of a place of utter weakness, and I knew it. I was exactly where Satan wanted me: a prisoner to a pain so deep that the only way I could cope was to pretend it wasn't there. Of course, denial never works in the long run.

I prayed and cried out to God, but the victory I sought eluded me. The attacks worsened. I was living two separate lives: one as the confident young wife of Jay St. John and the other as a little girl afraid of her own shadow.

During this time, my mom invited me to go with her to a Bible study at Hinson Memorial Baptist Church in Portland. Once a week, the group met to discuss a book that I still praise God for: *The Search for Significance* by Robert S. McGee. Throughout the pages of this book, I was challenged for the first time to see God's mercy as something I needed. I had grown so accustomed to pretending to be strong that the idea of receiving—let alone extending—mercy wasn't something I could even begin to understand.

The study also asked me to do something I wasn't used to doing: be honest. In the book, McGee offers this challenge to readers:

> Simply ask the Lord to give you the courage to be honest. Give Him permission to shine His Spirit's light on your thoughts, feelings, and actions. You may be surprised by additional pain as you realize the extent of your wounds, but our experience of healing can only be as deep as our awareness of the need for it. This takes the power of God's light. Ask Him to turn on the light.[1]

I read the last line again: "Ask Him to turn on the light." That night, alone in my bedroom, I knelt down and asked God to turn on the light. In the quiet of my heart, God met me, and a little night-light came on in my soul. God knows, I don't think I could have handled much more light than that at the time. My process of healing began with that little beam, and I realized I needed to learn to do two things: speak the truth and practice forgiveness. It wasn't perfect, but it was a start.

The road to wholeness was going to be a long one. Without even realizing it, I had let pain become my inner voice. It defined me. Anxiety was the first thing I experienced in the morning when my heart started racing and the last thing I felt at night before the Xanax took the edge off. Deep inside, I knew God required me to forgive, but it seemed like an unrealistic expectation, given the condition of my heart. At the end of the day, I was angry. Angry at God for allowing abuse in my life, and angry at myself for not being able to simply "forgive and forget."

It never occurred to me that I was choosing pain over freedom, bitterness over release. Bitterness was easy. I had a rationale for it. Forgiveness? Not so much. It didn't make sense. It didn't seem fair.

Unforgiveness is like kryptonite to your walk with God.

I didn't understand that unforgiveness was like kryptonite to my walk with God. So I stayed stuck there, a prisoner of my own unwillingness to step out of my past and allow God to heal the broken places in my heart. It would take becoming a mother to bring me to the place where I wanted to be victorious more than I wanted to be a victim.

LORD, HAVE MERCY

It was February 1991—the month I discovered I was pregnant with our first child. While I was excited to become a mother and I never once regretted our little "surprise," my pregnancy brought every fear, insecurity, and lie the devil had ever told me to the surface. Being pregnant meant I needed to confront my weaknesses head-on.

It also meant I needed to go off my anxiety medication. Bummer.

With very little in my arsenal to combat my continuing anxiety attacks, I found myself talking to God a lot more. Isn't it funny how we tend to do that? When I was fine, my prayer life suffered. It was only when I was in pain that it became more active. Fortunately, God is patient with us. There I was, shaking my fist at Him, and He was extending mercy to me. As I prayed, God began to show me that, while my hurt was real, it was also chaining me to my history. I needed to let go.

Becoming unchained required mercy. I wanted to lash out, to exact revenge. God was saying, *That's not your place. Have mercy.* I knew immediately that God was asking me to extend mercy to my dad. But after I became pregnant, I realized I had some pretty big issues with my mom, too. I wondered why she hadn't done a better job of keeping my brother and me safe. I couldn't understand the lies, the years of covering up our reality. That made me even more furious with her than I was with my dad. The little baby inside me proved to be a constant reminder of how absolutely unprotected I'd felt as a child. The more I thought about it, the angrier I got.

But God wouldn't let me go. I could hear Him whispering, *Forgive.*

"But Lord! You don't get it!"

Forgive.

I continued to struggle until one morning when, as I was quickly reading my Bible in a token quiet time, I read this verse:

God blesses those who are merciful,
for they will be shown mercy.

MATTHEW 5:7

As someone who grew up in church, I had read this verse and heard it preached in dozens of sermons. Up to that point, it had just been words to me, words that didn't carry any real significance. But now the words hit me in a new way. Blessed are the merciful, for they shall *be shown* mercy. I wanted mercy. God knew I needed it, and yet He was asking me to *give* mercy, not just seek it for myself. This was the first time I realized that sometimes mercy must be given in order to be received.

And that wasn't going to be easy. Choosing mercy meant I had to let go of the past. It meant I would need to forgive—really forgive—my parents for the years of abuse I had experienced when I was growing up. I asked the Lord to help me understand what this would look like. All I heard in response was one word: *Pray.*

Over the next several months, I began to pray in a different way for my parents. I prayed that God would give me the strength to forgive them. And to my surprise, the more mercy I offered, the more I received! Even though Satan had successfully choked the forgiveness out of my family when I was a child, I now was learning something I hadn't understood before. Satan can talk us into being unforgiving, but he can't stop us from extending forgiveness. And what's more, he can't block us from receiving it. Satan is no match for the healing and forgiveness God offers.

Satan is no match for the healing and forgiveness God offers.

Do you need to extend forgiveness to someone? MomStrong moms recognize that forgiveness is necessary if we're going to grow in the Lord. If we want to experience mercy, we need to offer forgiveness instead of withholding it. It's because of the Lord's faithfulness that we can dare to forgive and let go—and hope.

> Yet I still dare to hope
>   when I remember this:
> The faithful love of the LORD never ends!
>   His mercies never cease.
> Great is his faithfulness;
>   his mercies begin afresh each morning.
> LAMENTATIONS 3:21-23

THE SNARE OF BEING OFFENDED

At the risk of sounding a little preachy here, I actually looked something up in the original Greek. Did you know that the

Greek word for "offense" is *skandalon*, which literally means the part of an animal trap where bait is hung? In other words, an offense is literally a trap. Got it? Good. Because here's my point: if we're in a battle (and the Bible clearly says we are), it makes perfect sense that the devil would choose to use offenses to catch us in his snare. Satan lays all kinds of traps for us, and I'm convinced he hunts among the hurting. Think about it— when people offend us, we get angry and hold grudges. That leads to unforgiveness, which leads to broken relationships, which lead to self-pity and isolation, which lead to broken communication with God. From there, it's nothing but discouragement and defeat.

When we stop walking with God and stop seeking His strength, we're in danger of becoming like Samson at the hands of Delilah—weak and vulnerable. If our strength comes from the Lord and we aren't walking in right relationship with Him, our strength wanes. When we harbor offenses instead of letting go, we become weak.

When someone hurts you, you may think that the one with the greatest agenda for evil is the person who offended you. But in reality, there is a bigger spiritual agenda being played out here. Offense is one of the enemy's most powerful weapons, and its primary purpose is to keep us from growing in power and strength in the Lord. To render us ineffective. To take us off the battlefield and out of the war. To sideline us. To see us disengage with others who would make us more effective in the battle we're fighting.

We have to guard our hearts against being easily offended. It's a biblical truth that the pure in heart hear from God more readily than those who are full of bitterness: "Blessed are the

pure in heart: for they shall see God" (Matthew 5:8, KJV).
A heart that is full of offenses and unforgiveness isn't a pure
heart. If we want to hear from God, we have to refuse to allow
offenses to rule and reign in our lives. Even big ones. Even
abuse.

I'm not saying you should just excuse the terrible thing that
happened to you, as if it were no big deal, like someone forgetting to return your call. There's no question: forgiving the big
things is hard. But Jesus, who knows all too well the pain of
rejection, doesn't give us an option.

> I tell you the truth, you can say to this mountain, "May
> you be lifted up and thrown into the sea," and it will
> happen. But you must really believe it will happen and
> have no doubt in your heart. I tell you, you can pray
> for anything, and if you believe that you've received it,
> it will be yours. But when you are praying, first forgive
> anyone you are holding a grudge against, so that your
> Father in heaven will forgive your sins, too.
>
> MARK 11:23-25

Notice that even our prayers are hindered by an unwillingness
to forgive! Perhaps this is the reason God doesn't put any quali-
fiers on forgiveness. He doesn't say, "Well, that was a pretty bad
offense. You can hang on to that one." No. He says, in effect,
"Before you come to me and ask for things, you need to forgive anyone you're holding a grudge against." That's *anything*
against *anyone*. God's Word is clear: if we want Him to hear
us, we must not harbor unforgiveness in our hearts. We have
to get this right. Our children are watching.

MONKEY SEE, MONKEY DO

Writer and family counselor Dorothy Law Nolte opens her timeless poem "Children Learn What They Live" this way:

> *If children live with criticism, they learn*
> *to condemn.*
> *If children live with hostility, they learn*
> *to fight.*
> *If children live with fear, they learn to*
> *be apprehensive.*

She is absolutely right. We all grow up watching how the adults around us handle conflict. In my family, we had three options: ignore the conflict, run from it, or explode. As a young mother, I was living what I'd learned—and it was obvious. My first response to an offense was to be self-protective and ignore the person who offended me. If that didn't work, I reverted to the other two options I'd seen modeled by my family: I'd try to escape the problem or blow up at the other person. I had no forgiveness option or reset button.

When our children are young, we might have a hard time imagining the unintended consequences of unforgiveness. But let me assure you: they are very real. Unforgiveness wreaks havoc on us—body, mind, and spirit. What we model for our children can help keep them from devastating consequences—some of which we've experienced ourselves. Part of our job as mothers is to equip our kids to handle things better than we did, even as we're in the process of learning ourselves.

When I saw the pattern I was setting for my children early in their lives, I knew I needed to do better. I wanted more for our family than what I'd grown up with. For the first time in my life, I wanted to throw it all off—the anger, the bitterness, the unforgiveness. The prescription bottle stops here!

MomStrong moms model forgiveness for their children not only because God requires it but also because they want their children to be pure of heart, obedient to God, and strong for battle. I wish every mom understood the importance of forgiveness, especially since we're so easily offended in this age of political correctness. We can't afford to let Satan use the trap of offense to ensnare us any longer. We can't afford to allow our offenses to become stumbling blocks in our lives. Too much is at stake! If we as mothers can't teach our own children what forgiveness looks like, where will our culture be twenty years from now? It takes only one generation to change the course of the culture.[2] And if you'll forgive my boldness, I think that's pretty important.

WHEN FORGIVENESS SEEMS IMPOSSIBLE

Maybe for you, the pain seems too deep to forgive. Maybe the people who hurt you don't want to be forgiven. Maybe they don't care at all. Maybe you don't care anymore either. Sometimes it seems like more effort than it's worth, this business of forgiveness.

If that's how you feel, listen carefully. If you don't think you can forgive, you've been deceived. The enemy is lying to you. Don't listen to him.

There's something you need to understand about the nature of God: He won't ask you to do something that isn't within your power to do. For example, God isn't going to ask me to be a man. My chromosomes have been set, and there's nothing I can do to change my DNA. Just as we have certain qualities that are set in our DNA, we have set qualities in our spiritual DNA as well. The ability to forgive is in the DNA of every born-again Christian. That means that when God asks us to forgive, it *is* within our power to do it. Why? Because of the indwelling power of the Holy Spirit! Our power to forgive doesn't come from within us; it comes from God.

> *The ability to forgive is in the DNA of every born-again Christian.*

Now you may never hear the words "I'm sorry" from the person who caused you pain. And while it may feel good to hold on to unforgiveness for a while, eventually that resentment will eat you alive. It gives power to the devil and to the person who hurt you. So if the person you're struggling to forgive hasn't asked you for forgiveness, forgive them anyway. I know firsthand that this is not easy, but it's worth it. Do it for yourself and for your family. You can do it. You must!

I've heard it said that hanging on to unforgiveness is like swallowing poison and expecting the other person to die. When unforgiveness settles into the soul of the human heart, bitterness moves in too. Like bacteria in a petri dish, bitterness thrives in the heart of the unforgiving person—and eventually it will destroy you.

Years ago, a wise sister in Christ noticed that I couldn't let go of the frustration and hurt I'd been harboring in the wake of a disagreement with a former friend. It had been bothering me for ages, and over time I became bitter. One day in a moment of Holy Spirit–directed boldness, my friend said, "Heidi, I've heard you talking about this for a long time. I've heard you praying about it. Since you're not getting the reconciliation your heart desires, it's time to let go. To do that, you have to stop thinking about it. Stop talking about it. Stop giving it power. Don't worry about the other person. Instead, focus on your family and move forward."

My friend was so wise. Her words showed me that forgiveness doesn't mean allowing an untrustworthy person into a relationship with us. It doesn't mean we automatically invite the person who was reckless with our emotions back into our lives. Sometimes we can. But sometimes the healthy thing to do is untangle the rope that's tying our hurt to another person's life and move forward . . . before bitterness sets up shop.

> *God will always provide us with a strength equal to the task He's calling us to.*

MomStrong moms guard their hearts against bitterness and unforgiveness. Be the mom who doesn't hold back love for fear of being hurt or rejected. Through the power of the Holy Spirit, you can refuse to let your past rob you and your family of the future God has for you. He has so much more for you than the devil wants you to believe. God, ever true to His Word, will always provide us with a strength equal to the task He's calling us to. The ability to forgive is available to us, if we simply ask. In fact, the work of forgiveness is already completed in Jesus—we need only to take hold of it.

MOM**STRONG** MOM, LET GO AND LIVE FREE!

The first time I tiptoed into telling the truth about my past was at a small women's conference in Baltimore, Maryland. When the conference was over, several women came up to talk to me. I was amazed at their response to my story. Many of the women identified with my experiences, but what surprised me most was a comment made by a woman who had followed me on social media for many years. "I had no idea you came from such a difficult background!" she said. "You seem so full of joy!"

Do you know what? I am full of joy—because my spirit has been set free from worrying about whether so-and-so deserved to be forgiven. Precious mom, forgiveness brings freedom. It's amazing what God can do with us when we refuse to remain tied to the actions of the person who hurt us.

Do you want to be MomStrong? Then learn to forgive. By God's good design, forgiveness and healing go hand in hand. Move forward, mom! Don't let something from your past keep you from the future God has planned for you.

Forgive. Lean in to God's promises. Let go of your past hurts. Live free.

PRAYER POINTS FOR A
MOM WHO IS FREE

- Pray that God will release you from any unforgiveness you are holding on to from your childhood (see Matthew 6:15).
- Pray that God will free you from any offenses that are hindering you in your walk with Him (see Proverbs 19:11).
- Pray that your children will learn to extend mercy to those who hurt them (see Matthew 5:7).

Chapter 8

INTO THE LIGHT

*I*n the 1939 classic film *The Wizard of Oz*, Dorothy and her friends are startled to discover that "the great and powerful" wizard who has kept the entire land of Oz captivated by his strength and wisdom is, in reality, a frail little man hiding behind a curtain.

In today's age of TMI, you'd think we wouldn't have this problem anymore, but from what I can see, we're hiding more now than ever. Many moms today are doing exactly what the wizard did: hiding behind a curtain. Granted, our curtains look more like computer screens, but if we're honest, I think a lot of us can identify with the wizard. I know I can.

As you know by now, I grew up behind a curtain that masked

domestic violence and fear. Though I put up a good front, the truth was that my dad, whose father was an abusive alcoholic, had become an abusive man himself. While we looked like a wonderful Christian family on the surface, my home life was very different behind the curtain. My mother, my siblings, and I lived with threats (spoken and unspoken) of impending disaster, never knowing what would set off the next fit of rage and violence. Sure, people tried to help. Neighbors called the police to our home on a number of occasions, but in an attempt to maintain what little peace we could for the 97 percent of the time when the police weren't there, we smiled and gave the appearance that everything was fine. I became good at making excuses for bruises and other minor injuries. I learned to lie. *That's what you do when you're afraid.*

By the way, fear is a terrible houseguest for many reasons, but one undeniable reason is that it likes to keep us in the dark. Fear's best friend—Satan—is a liar. In fact, he's the father of lies (see John 8:44), and lies flourish—you guessed it—in darkness: both spiritual darkness, which frames a wrong understanding of grace and the gospel, and emotional darkness, which disguises a lack of grace toward ourselves and others (ungrace) as love. The only antidote to this darkness is authenticity.

I've observed that, for the most part, society doesn't value being authentic—unless it means you can embrace "your" truth. What is that, anyway? Your truth, my truth? Truth, by its nature, is *what matches reality.* And yet, I'm watching a generation of women *who know right from wrong* but who are afraid to bring truth into the light. Why? Fear. Remember, fear always accompanies a lie. When you live with fear, it becomes normal to lie. Lies don't have to be malicious, you know. Most of the time, we lie simply because the truth is too painful to face. I lied about my family because I was afraid of what would happen to me if my dad found out that I told the truth—but we can lie about other things too.

For example, I've lied about how much time I spend online: *I'm not really spending too much time on social media.* Sound familiar, even benign? It's meant to. The devastating truth about spending too much time online is that it's usually not discovered until the stakes are higher and the kids are older. Occasionally, when we're *really* afraid, we lie about how we feel when another mom seems to be succeeding where we're struggling. We lie to ourselves as a means of protection. We lie to hide weakness and mask failure, but here's the thing: truth is necessary if we're going to face life's challenges from a position of strength. We must learn to live our lives in the light of God's Word.

If you're hiding even one foot behind a curtain today, this is for you: the devil wants this generation of moms to be stuck, not strong, and he knows that the antidote to being stuck can only be found in truth. Just like the wizard needed to be seen in the light for who he was in order to be restored, we also need to allow ourselves to be seen—not so that we can wallow in our past, but so that we can move beyond it. If your mothering has been less than you wanted it to be up until now, if your online life looks more like a Dumpster fire on Facebook than a platform to offer encouragement and truth—then it's time. Link arms with people who will love you enough to tell you the truth about your life. Invest in friendships with women who are not afraid to bring you into the light. Jesus said, "I am the way, the truth, and the life" (John 14:6). Life is found in the light of truth, and truth is found in the Word of God.

Of course, I'm making it sound easier than it is to hear truth. If you're a "truth teller"—a person who sees things in tones of black and white—allow this fellow truth teller to gently remind you of something that I have learned the hard way: truth can't be heard when it takes on the harsh tones of ungrace—and it can't be given from a place of legalistic rhetoric if it's going have any chance of getting past fear. We've got to package truth in love.

We've got to package truth in love.

LOVE IS GONNA KEEP US ALIVE

I still smile when I remember the way God packaged my favorite truth teller. He was wearing pink Converse tennis shoes and a yellow Generra shirt and was sporting a classic '80s mullet when he skateboarded into my life.

Jay St. John was the lead singer of a local Christian rock-and-roll band appropriately named Saint John, so of course he made it his ambition to woo me with his unique blend of Journey-like electric guitar solos and his soft tenor voice. It was a brilliant strategy—this mix of mullet and music!

Mullet aside, Jay's tender heart for others and love for God captivated me. After a few visits to Escape from New York Pizza in downtown Portland, Oregon, I knew I had found someone special. Luckily for me, he felt the same way, and we decided to start dating.

I love my memories of our early years together. Underneath his rock-and-roll style, Jay was quiet and thoughtful—the perfect foil to my extroverted personality and hidden insecurities. Jay saw a side of me that most people didn't, and I loved him for it. He shone a light of truth on what he observed, even when he knew it was hard for me to face. He didn't run when he realized that my family wasn't as healthy as we tried to appear. Yes, Jay was up for the fight of his life—and he got it when he asked me to be his wife.

In the spring of 1989, after a few months of premarital counseling and after writing out several lists of marriage pros and cons, we decided that the pro column looked pretty good. Jay proposed, and we got hitched just six months later, on a hot day in late September. I was just nineteen, and he was twenty-one. We were babies, of course, but we didn't know it then.

The classic Eagles song "Love Will Keep Us Alive" summed it up well. After the wedding I continued night classes at Multnomah University while Jay worked full-time to finish his degree. Like many young married couples, we lived on rice and beans, but we didn't mind. Besides, we were going to make it in music. And if the band couldn't pay the bills, we figured the pastorate would. (Insert Eagles song again. Yeah, we sang that a lot. It's a good thing, too, because you need to know that song if you decide to marry a pastor.)

THE WOMAN BEHIND THE CURTAIN

While at Multnomah, I had the privilege of attending Spiritual Life 101 once a week under the instruction of an amazingly tender, godly teacher, Dr. John Mitchell. He was in his early nineties when I first heard him speak on suffering.

One morning, in a huge auditorium filled with eager Bible students, Dr. Mitchell asked a simple question: "Do you want to serve the Savior?" His words echoed in my ears. He had a slight Irish accent, and I remember smiling as I raised my hand high, along with all the other would-be shepherds of the next generation. Then while our hands were still high in the air, Dr. Mitchell paused, stepped slightly away from the lectern, and looked out into the room.

"Before God will use you greatly," he said, "He will wound you deeply. Are you ready to be pruned by the Master?"

Several hands, including mine, slowly went down. Of course, it wasn't because I didn't want to follow Jesus; it was because I hadn't considered there might be a cost involved. Dr. Mitchell's words fell heavy on my heart. I'm sure he summed up his message masterfully, but I don't remember hearing much else after that. I simply couldn't imagine being pruned any more.

I had come to faith in Christ at a young age. I loved Him. I believed His story. I'd felt just a portion of His amazing grace and *thought* that I had experienced the depths of His power, but at that point in my life, I realize now, I knew *nothing* about His healing. You see, my picture of God was based on what I knew of my own earthly father. I pictured God as a cold, authoritarian figure, just waiting to punish me when I missed the mark. The God I knew may have sent Jesus, but He didn't love the way Jesus did. He was all about the bottom line. Right or wrong, heaven or hell, all or nothing.

To me, God's "pruning" was reckless and without purpose—and I figured I'd had enough of that in my life already. I didn't understand that God wanted to shine His light into the broken places in my heart to show me that His strength could be made perfect there. Because of my pride, the last thing I wanted was to be seen as weak.

God wants to shine His light into the broken places in your heart to show you that His strength is made perfect in weakness.

Because I didn't trust God's heart toward me, I had no intention of allowing Him anywhere near me with His divine pruning shears. *Pruned by the Master?* I thought. *No, thanks.*

Sitting in that auditorium, I had a crisis of belief. My hands were cold and clammy. My heart raced, and my stomach was tied in knots. The thought that God would ask more of me than had already been required seemed impossible to take in. If surrendering to Him meant I'd have to face more pain, I was sure I didn't have anything left to offer Him.

I closed my notebook and went home. And for the next twelve hours, I cried. When I arrived at work the following morning, a few of my coworkers noticed my puffy eyes.

"Hey, are you okay, Heidi?" my friend Carrie asked.

"I'm fine," I lied. "Just a little tired."

Even at my weakest, I held the curtain securely in place. It was what I knew. Get things done. Be happy. Impress people. Smile. Be the best. Work harder. Pretend. But pretending is part of what happens when we are too afraid to let the light in. And it can last for only so long.

In the days that followed, Professor Mitchell's words kept coming back to me. "Before God will use you greatly, He will wound you deeply." I trusted Dr. Mitchell. This wasn't theoretical for him—he knew pain personally. As a man in his nineties, he knew something that it takes most people a lifetime to learn: that often our greatest ministry comes out of our deepest hurts.

People suffer every day, but it's not the suffering that's transformative. Transformation happens when we allow God's truth to shine onto our suffering. It's what we do with suffering that ends up having an impact in this world. Think about it. Who better to minister to a woman battling breast cancer than a woman who has undergone chemo and a mastectomy? Who can touch the heart of a mother mourning the loss of a child better than a woman who has walked that road herself? No one can understand the pain of child abuse like someone who has also walked that long road to wholeness herself.

What Dr. Mitchell was trying to teach us can be summed up in one small but mighty word: trust. Do you trust God? Just like a master gardener prunes with purpose, He does too. He is in the business of pruning people: taking a rough, untamed heart and transforming it into the image of His Son. God's heart toward us can be clearly seen in the book of Romans:

> We know that God causes everything to work together for the good of those who love God and are called according to his purpose for them. ROMANS 8:28

The Bible says that *everything* works together for good for those who are called according to His purpose. *In other words:* if God allows it, it's for a purpose. And though it may hurt like nobody's business, nothing can change the truth of God's promises to us or His heart toward us. His heart is good; His purposes are good. Realizing this challenged and eventually changed my perspective on the purpose of suffering. In God's economy, everything, even pain, has purpose. This is an important truth for moms to realize—because sometimes our greatest suffering may be in sharing the pain our children experience. God sees it all the same.

Looking back, I realize that the grief I walked through during those childhood years was a gift. According to God, my pain wasn't without meaning. The *truth*, as it turned out, was just as God promised in Romans 8:28. He wanted to use it for His glory. My story, His glory.

Your pain isn't without meaning. God wants to use it for His glory.

Ever true to His Word, God didn't waste my tears, and He won't waste yours. If you're struggling with past pain, precious mom, take it to the One who is acquainted with grief. If your child is suffering and you doubt God's goodness, shine the light of Romans 8:28 like a flashlight into your soul. God has you in His grasp—and He has your children, too.

Rather than let your past determine your future, rather than allow your pain to determine your present, allow God to use these things for good. God will use your pain for His purposes in wonderful ways that will bring beauty from ashes as you trust Him. I promise.

Better yet, He promises.

NEW EVERY MORNING

In an effort to compensate for my insecurities, I became the consummate people pleaser. This eventually escalated to the point where the very thought of offending anyone set my heart racing. My cries for help were stifled by pride that masqueraded as confidence. I longed for strength but found weakness. I was aware that something inside of me was in need of healing, but I was too scared to let anyone see behind the curtain long enough to find it.

When, after eighteen months of married life, I learned that I was pregnant, my panic and fear escalated. I needed someone to turn on the light and tell me the truth about who I was if I was going to navigate motherhood with any hope of success. I needed another mom in my life.

My anxiety reached a boiling point when I was in my thirty-eighth week of pregnancy. Jay and I had just finished our last childbirth education class—you know, the one where they tell you that if you breathe right it won't hurt. Yeah, that one.

One by one, the women got up to leave and passed Nola, our childbirth educator, on the way to the door. Nola hugged the sweet mamas and kissed their tummies as they left, making sure to give each of the dads-to-be a high five as she assured them that all would be well.

We liked Nola. We knew her from church, and the past few weeks had given me confidence that she was someone I could be real with. *Maybe, just maybe,* I thought, *she can help.*

I waited until there was no one else left in the room before

I made eye contact with her. When she sat down next to me, I couldn't hold my tears back. As I stared at my big, full-term belly, I began to cry. "I'm afraid! I can't do this!" I sobbed.

"You're going to be fine," she said, her eyes soft and comforting. "Your body was made for this."

Of course, she had no idea that birthing the baby wasn't what I feared. My fears went much deeper. They threatened our future as a family and robbed me of peace. My father's profound disappointment in who I was had shaped the way I saw myself and convinced me I was destined to fail.

I felt weak. I feared I couldn't be the kind of mom I wanted to be. I feared I was destined to give my child the same upbringing I'd had. I feared I would lose my temper, even to the point of injuring the precious baby I carried. But worse than all these, I feared my baby would grow to fear me the way I had feared my father. Behind the curtain, I was almost desperate for someone else to be this baby's mom.

As I cried, the curtain lifted, and—one little piece at a time—all my weaknesses were exposed for Nola to see. And that's when it happened: God met me. There, in my weakness, He met me.

Nola laid her hands on my belly and looked at me. Her heart seemed to ache with mine. "Oh, Heidi!" she said. "Don't you know who you are? You are new! God has made you new! You are a new creation, and your baby is the beginning of the healing that is coming, if you'll let God shine His love into the deep places in your heart. You. Are. New. Do you believe that?"

I wanted to believe it. I was desperate for God. I cried out to Him, aware that something inside me was beginning to break free. In that moment, when I let just one other person see the woman behind the curtain, God began a healing in my life that continues to this day. I didn't fully understand what Nola meant at the time, but I knew I needed to cling to Jesus. If I was going to be strong for my child, I needed to accept my weakness as an opportunity to find God's strength. I needed that strength to invade my heart, to comfort and heal me.

Driving home that night, my faith began to take on new meaning. For the first time, I began to believe that God could heal a generational sin in my family. I knew that the only chance my daughter had of being whole was for me to cling to my Creator. God was calling me out from behind the curtain and into the light.

A few weeks later, after twenty-six hours of labor, our daughter Savannah was born. No feeling in the world can compare to the wave of emotions that wash over a mother when she sees her child for the very first time. Instantly, this little girl held my heart. I was captivated by her simplest movements, and I loved the way she looked at me. As I looked at her, something stood out to me that other mothers might not appreciate: *my daughter was not afraid.* Her heart was as open toward me as mine was toward her. It was miraculous.

God was using the miracle of motherhood to open my eyes. I began to see God's love for me in a new way. I'd never experienced such raw love. As I stared at my daughter's beautiful newborn features and marveled at her every movement, I sensed God whispering, *This is how I see you.* On frustrating nights when the baby wouldn't sleep and exhaustion threatened to undo me, I clung to the promises of a Father who loved me unconditionally. He said, "My mercies will be new again tomorrow" (see Lamentations 3:22-23).

And they were.

THE STRENGTH OF AUTHENTICITY

I have come to believe that many of our struggles as mothers are rooted in the past. Some of us grew up in circumstances that made us feel vulnerable and afraid, so we struggle with the need to control everything around us in an attempt to feel protected. Some of us were bullied as children, and we struggle with self-hatred. Others battle constant fear and anxiety. We all have something that brings us to the end of ourselves. Regardless of our unique circumstances, when we peel back the layers of self-protection, we quickly discover that we are all in need of a Savior.

MomStrong moms are okay with needing help because they know it's not a bad thing to be weak. After all, weakness is where we discover how strong God is. It's where His strength is found.

As women, we relate to the story of the little man behind the curtain because we all have a tendency to hide the way he did. The wizard's problem wasn't that he was incapable—quite the opposite! He was the ruler of a grand city, but he was afraid of what people would think if they saw him for what he really was: short and socially awkward, with an affinity for mechanics. He was a prisoner of his own fears and insecurities, and he desperately needed someone to shine some light behind his grand facade. His experience was much like ours.

And although my experience may not be exactly like yours, my hunch is that our stories aren't that different. After all, women have been hiding behind curtains for generations. The image of the "perfect housewife" from the '40s and '50s often covered alcohol abuse and infidelity. The '60s and '70s saw culture swinging from legalism to liberty, and eventually, in a no-holds-barred attempt to gain a sense of self and freedom, women burned their bras and gave away free love, only to end up disillusioned.

Solomon was right. Truly, there is "nothing new under the sun" (Ecclesiastes 1:9, NIV). The fact that we hide isn't new, although the things we hide behind might be. Today many of us hide behind a screen. The Internet is like a giant curtain, and in front of it, everyone can be an expert. Everyone can be strong. Brad Paisley summed it up perfectly in "Online," a song about a young man who is pretending to be someone else through his online persona:

I grow another foot,
And I lose a bunch of weight every time I log in.

As a blogger, I've seen this reality firsthand, as many wives and mothers I meet find themselves in a desperate search for significance amid a growing sea of voices. Having a "platform" is what's coveted now, and many mothers are losing their families in order to find it.

MomStrong moms know that authentic living doesn't need a platform; it *is* the platform. Our children see the real mom. The only platform they're concerned about is the one we're raising them on—and it needs to be authentic. The real thing happens when we honor God's priorities. That's worth working for and worth protecting.

So come out from behind the curtain, precious mom. Shine the light of God's truth into your situation, and let God show you how strong He really is. He's strong enough to handle whatever you're facing—and He carries a really big flashlight. It's big enough to light your way.

A PROMISE FULFILLED

One of the reasons I love God's Word so much is that it's filled with stories of people who found God's strength in the midst of their own weakness. They went from weak to strong because they trusted in God and realized somewhere along the line that *spiritual ends require spiritual means.* In other words: we've got to get serious about getting to know God. He's in the business of taking ordinary people with flaws and fears like yours and mine and pulling off miracles.

While the world scoffs at weakness, God uses it to sanctify us. All through the Bible, we see God's strength at its best when people are at their weakest. He took Joseph from a pit to a palace, He transformed Gideon from an ordinary man plagued by fear to a judge over Israel, and He used less-than-desirable circumstances to turn Esther from an obscure teenager into the queen of Persia. God is in the miracle business!

While the world scoffs at weakness, God uses it to sanctify us.

My life is a miracle too. It has been almost twenty-six years since that car ride home from Nola's house, and today my baby— the baby who was a catalyst for God's healing transformation in my life—is a mother herself. When I held my grandson for the first time, God's promise came back to my mind. Once again, His mercies were being made new for my family. His promise held true not only for me but for another generation.

If you're a woman living in fear behind a curtain, I challenge you to step out from behind it. Look your fears and weaknesses in the face, and declare these truths with me. You are new! You were born to be free, born to know the One who desires to be a "lamp unto [your] feet and a light unto [your] path" (Psalm 119:105, KJV). God is in the business of restoring broken people—of making the blind see, the lame walk, and the weak strong (see Matthew 11:5)—and He is rewriting your story the same way He is rewriting mine.

God is in the business of restoring broken people.

I understand now what Dr. Mitchell meant when he taught us about being pruned by the Master. God, the ultimate multitasker, is pruning you with your children in mind! He's preparing your children to bear fruit for His purposes, even as He strengthens and steadies you.

MOM**STRONG** MOM,
DARE TO LIVE AUTHENTICALLY

So how do we come through the pain of pruning and walk away from fear and into the light? We focus on becoming. Focusing on the big picture—on the work God is doing to transform us rather than on the temporary pain we feel—allows us to press in and move forward. "We do this by keeping our eyes on Jesus, the champion who initiates and perfects our faith" (Hebrews 12:2).

We all have to endure hardship and pain in this life. When we endure, what we're really doing is outlasting the enemy long enough to let the master pruner do what He needs to do in our lives for His glory. The Lord is a master gardener. If you let Him, He'll use your past and your pain to produce fruit far beyond what you could ask or imagine. Remember, God's tender pruning in your life isn't just for your benefit; it's for the good of your children and grandchildren, too.

So come out from behind the curtain, precious mom, and into the light. Dare to live authentically. You can trust that the pruning is for a purpose. Though the process is painful, you can trust Him. He will never leave or forsake you. You have His Word on it!

PRAYER POINTS FOR AN
AUTHENTIC MOM

- Pray that you will be able to pull back the curtain and be authentic with God and at least one other person about your past hurts (see James 5:16).
- Pray that you will be open to the Lord's pruning and that you will come out stronger as a result (see Hebrews 12:2).
- Pray that any generational curses in your family will be broken (see Deuteronomy 7:9).

Chapter 9

NO-DRAMA MAMA

I knew when I "vague-booked" that little hint on my Facebook page that so-and-so would eventually get it. And secretly I hoped it would be sooner rather than later. I wanted her to know she'd hurt me. If I were being honest, I'd have to admit that I wanted to wound her back. The more I licked my wounds, the angrier I got. Forget about listening to that "still, small voice." I was too busy planning how I could get back at this person and still keep my Christian reputation intact.

I knew that if I called her out by name online, I'd be fouled on a technicality—because that would *clearly* be wrong—so I did what any reasonable, mature, Spirit-filled woman would do: I hinted about it on Facebook. Just a short statement. It looked innocent on the outside, but truthfully it was *anything* but innocent.

I came up with several variations of "take that" in my head before I landed on the perfect mixture of "Christianese" and "wounded warrior." Then out it tumbled, for all the online community to see:

Lord, help me to have a forgiving heart.

Mature, right? A prayer, even! Nice touch. Even now, I'm not sure what I was thinking. Whatever it was, it wasn't smart—that's for sure. Trust me when I say that having seven children can generate enough drama in a day to seriously cripple most human beings. I didn't need to invite Drama and her close friend, Discord, into my home. But for some reason I did it anyway.

> *Don't invite Drama and her close friend, Discord, into your home.*

As you can probably guess, my plan backfired. It backfired for several reasons, but the biggest one was this: the so-and-so I was talking about . . . was my mom.

As you know by now, my mom and I have been through our share of valleys over the course of our relationship. At the time of the dreaded Facebook post, we were actually in a pretty good place, but something she said hit me the wrong way. The next thing I knew, old hurts bubbled to the surface. She nicked an emotional scab that hadn't fully healed, and rather than risk losing in a confrontation with her, I decided to be mature about it and post a thinly veiled sarcastic response online.

Yeah. It didn't work.

Worse yet? She called me. You know, on the phone. Like a grown-up. It was weird.

"Heidi?" my mom began. "If you have something to say to me, I wish you would just call me."

Sure . . . I suppose I *could* have done that. But Facebooking about it seemed safer, easier, and just as effective.

I cringed. How had I sunk back to junior high level *with my own mother*? At least she had the good sense to call me out on it. The fact that I was a grown woman with several children of my own just made me look more foolish.

Don't you just *hate* it when Mom is right?

#toldyouso

I could have called my mom and admitted I was wounded, but now I had the added stress of embarrassment over the way I'd handled the situation. On top of that, I had a knot in my stomach that came from knowing my mom was—and had every right to be—hurt by my public display of frustration. Even though my post was written to an anonymous person, it wasn't anonymous to her. She knew—and I knew.

I thought of my own children. This wasn't the example I wanted to set for them.

Growing up in a dysfunctional, abusive environment had hardwired me to respond to confrontation in unhealthy ways. My first strategy was to avoid it at all costs. If that didn't work, I used the tried-and-true method of manipulating the other person into seeing things my way. Clearly, I didn't know what healthy confrontation looked like.

I had learned a painful untruth from my parents: it's easier to hide (literally and figuratively) than it is to risk coming out the loser. Manipulation feels safer. And really, that's what I was doing: I was hiding. Maybe you're hiding too. (By the way, if you're reading this and you happened to see that Facebook status all those years ago and wondered if it was about you, I apologize.)

It's embarrassing to admit that I acted in such a juvenile way, and I wouldn't bring it up for any other reason than this: I want us to do better. We *have* to do better. Our children need to learn how to wisely handle this brave new world of social media and the instant access it gives us to people's feelings and (what used to be) private struggles. Unfortunately, rude behavior has become commonplace on social media. I see it in grown women (including mothers like me) all the time.

It helps a little to know that we've been prone to this kind of behavior since the Garden of Eden. Eve was given instructions from God Himself about what she could and couldn't do in that amazing garden. It was simple, really: she should stay away from the tree of the knowledge of good and evil. But like me, with my foolish decision to call my mom out on Facebook, Eve just had to test God's resolve—you know, to see if her sin really would result in something awful. Think of the drama Eve's deception invited into all humankind! It's been nothing but drama ever since.

Like Eve, most of us know how God would have us live, but we're faced with temptations to live otherwise multiple times a day. The Internet has provided our generation with newer and greater opportunities to invite unnecessary conflict and drama into our homes. And while we can't filter out *all* the drama and strife we encounter on a daily basis, we can definitely do better at detecting and deflecting unnecessary drama.

The Internet has provided our generation with newer and greater opportunities to invite unnecessary conflict and drama into our homes.

If you're nodding, keep reading, because I believe we can handle our conflict more wisely—and set our children on a path to handling their own strife better than we have. There are no guarantees, of course, but emotionally healthy moms have a much better chance of instilling emotional health into their own children, too. It all starts at home. We've got to be honest about our underlying issue. What is it? See if you can relate:

ADDICTED TO DRAMA

Hi. My name is Heidi, and I'm a recovering drama addict. (See? Was that so hard?)

Like any addict, a drama addict usually needs a good, hard lesson about the pitfalls of being an addict in order to quit. Now I could go on and on about mistakes I've made in my relationships with other women over the years—hills I died on that in hindsight were relatively unimportant, words I said that caused hurt when I should have spoken words of healing, and conversations I engaged in that did more harm than good. But enough about me.

When I finally decided I wanted to get off the drama train, certain things became clearer for me. The first thing I noticed was that people who are addicted to drama actually invite it into their lives. They can't wait to tell you about their unkind friend or their nasty relative. The other thing I noticed was that almost 100 percent of gossip-based drama is negative in nature. So at the risk of sounding like a prosperity preacher, let me just say this: negative thoughts and words eventually bring about negative results.

People who are addicted to drama actually invite it into their lives.

See if you can recognize any of the telltale signs of a drama addict. Drama addicts

- insert themselves into situations where their presence isn't necessary or warranted,
- get people stirred up over things that are of little to no significance,
- "need" to know about relationships that aren't their own,
- live in the past,
- are in pain, and
- believe (or at least claim) that their motives for stirring up drama are pure (e.g., "I just want to help!").

Recognize anyone from that list? Recognize yourself? If so, it's time to get off the drama train. Be a no-drama mama! Moms today have enough on their plates without adding unnecessary drama to the list.

Maybe it's the fact that I'm well into my forties now, but I think I finally understand the value of pursuing peace. These days I actually *don't want to know* why so-and-so and what's-her-name from the co-op aren't speaking to each other anymore. I don't have the emotional energy for such talk, but more important, God says it's not pleasing to Him. Proverbs 21:23 makes the consequences of meddling clear: "Those who guard their mouths and their tongues keep themselves from calamity" (NIV).

Did you catch that? *Calamity.*

Hey, don't look at me. God said it—I didn't. Calamity is the sure result when we fail to control our tongues. The Word of God says over and over that our words have power: life or death is in the tongue.

> The tongue can bring death or life;
> those who love to talk will reap the consequences.
>
> PROVERBS 18:21

Solomon, who is considered one of the wisest people who ever lived, knew a thing or two about the power of the tongue. Listen to his admonition:

> Those who control their tongue will have a long life;
> opening your mouth can ruin everything.
>
> PROVERBS 13:3

Those who guard their tongues preserve their lives. 'Nuff said—in theory. But the truth is, even though we know better, we still have trouble controlling our tongues. So what is it about this issue that hits every woman at her core?

In this age of reality TV, we're rapidly becoming addicted to having TMI about other people. And how can we avoid the information overload? The gossip-driven, drama-rich culture of the "real housewives" of New Jersey and Beverly Hills has made its way to ordinary households across the country. It's not new, really. I mean, all you have to do is look back at the story of Abraham's wife, Sarah, and her servant, Hagar. Sarah actually *asked* Hagar to sleep with her husband, Abraham, because, after all, all the other men's wives were bearing children for their husbands. We seem to be wired for competition, not contentment—but God says we can be content as long as we're looking to Him and not to others to find the measure of our worth.

Yes, drama happens everywhere, but fortunately, we get to decide whether we will participate or walk away. If you want to become MomStrong, then I encourage you, for the sake of your sanity and for the sake of your children, to walk away. Walk away carefully, though. Don't get all hyperspiritual about it and announce that you're walking away because you're holier than your friends. Behavior like that will land you in good company with the Pharisees. Remember them? They wanted everyone to know that they were *better* than everyone else. Don't replace unrighteous behavior with self-righteous behavior. In situations like this, actions are what count. Just walk away.

You may not feel like you have the inner strength to avoid drama, but take heart—you don't have to do this alone. When we listen for the Holy Spirit, He will guide our words and our actions. We can learn to live in such a way that we sense God's hand on our shoulders (or in my case, over my mouth!) whenever we're tempted to stir up or engage in drama. When we walk with the Spirit, He tells us when to speak up and when to be quiet. He's good like that. So when you sense God saying, *This isn't for you,* quietly excuse yourself.

That's right—walk away. There's nothing to say (or listen to) here.

Bottom line: if we want our kids to be disciplined in the art of recognizing and avoiding drama, we have to be able to do it first ourselves. The greatest motherhood challenge is to discipline yourself to know when to walk away. Believe me: it's better that way. If you choose the path of discipline, you won't have to live with the sting of regret.

HOW TO RECOGNIZE A DIVISIVE SPIRIT

The United States recently survived one of the most divisive presidential elections in the history of the country. All over Facebook, friends were "unfriending" each other over things with no eternal significance. At the height of the hoopla, a friend of mine wisely observed, "Someone needs to bring some sanity to Facebook! It's like a Dumpster fire on there!" He was right—along with the people who were easily offended, there were also people who liked offending others, intentionally pouring emotional "gasoline" into the Dumpster! It was an embarrassing time in our nation's history. Fortunately, all is not lost. We can, and should, learn something from the Dumpster fire, because the same things we saw playing out on social media are playing out in the church today.

Years ago, when Jay was pastoring, we dealt with a difficult situation that involved a divisive couple. Now divisive people aren't always easy to spot, but one telltale sign is that they often come across as wanting to be helpful when in actuality they love to create strife. Key word here: *love*. They thrive on stirring things up. Believe me, the *d* in drama is for "divisive."

We learned the hard way that divisiveness within a community eventually spells heartbreak and trouble. This couple showed up in the early stages when we planted a homeschool ministry in the Pacific Northwest. They arrived on the scene with all kinds of great ideas and lots of enthusiasm. They seemed eager to help. We made a critical mistake when, instead of taking the time to get to know them, we put them in a position of leadership. Several months later, we discovered that they were unhappy with a decision we'd made. Rather than coming to us directly, they went to a group of parents who were involved in the ministry and stirred up trouble, making the whole situation tense.

My husband went to the couple and explained that if they had questions or issues with the way we were running the ministry, we would be happy to hear about them. Jay also reminded them that it was harmful to take their complaints to others before bringing them to us. Unfortunately, their divisive behavior continued. Whenever we left town, they would send the group e-mails that openly questioned our authority and in which they offered to start a new group, thereby dividing what had once been a cohesive group of families. How we wish we'd asked God for wisdom before putting them into a position of authority!

Eventually, we had to ask them to leave our organization. It took years to heal the wounds they left behind, both personally and in our ministry. I wish we'd known the danger of divisiveness then, and more than that, I wish we'd heeded the apostle Paul's instructions regarding divisive people:

> If people are causing divisions among you, give a first and second warning. After that, have nothing more to do with them. TITUS 3:10

It's the original "three strikes and you're out" rule, and every mom who wants to avoid drama should take note. Drama does nothing but tear down families, relationships, churches, and ministries. As Jesus taught us, a house divided against itself cannot stand (see Matthew 12:25; Mark 3:25).

As a pastor's wife for nearly twenty years, I've seen a number of divisive people. I've even been divisive myself, which has put me in the awkward position of needing to ask for forgiveness for my actions. The problem is that most of the time, a divisive person will tell you they aren't what you say they are. You need to be discerning. Here's an example: someone has been hurt by another Christian. Instead of taking their concern directly *to* that person, they broadcast it to everyone else. Rather than showing concern for the body of Christ and handling the matter in private, where it belongs, they put on a public display of self-righteousness in an attempt to shame the other person and make themselves look better.

One of the most common themes in the New Testament is that of unity. In Ephesians 4:3, Paul instructs the church to "make every effort to keep yourselves united in the Spirit, binding yourselves together with peace." God cares about His children living in right relationship with Him and with each other. Divisive people put an end to that unity. So be on guard, precious mom. This is not a reality show.

FIVE WAYS TO GET (AND STAY) DRAMA-FREE

The Bible makes it clear that God wants us to find peace amid the important relationships in our lives. Yet opportunities to stray outside His peace abound. Even prayer groups (where gossip is often justified under the guise of prayer requests) can turn sour if we're not careful.

MomStrong moms know how to say no to drama. Here are a few tips to help:

1. **Listen.** We need to become better listeners. Women are nurturers by nature, but in this age of iPhones and computers, texting and tablets, we're losing touch with the art of listening. The goal of listening should always be to understand where the other person is coming from, not to formulate your next comeback or zinger. When both parties want to understand each other, relationships flourish and drama is rare. We also need to listen to that still, small voice that whispers to us when we're writing those drama-inviting posts on Facebook or passing along gossip. You know, *that* voice—the little check you feel in your spirit when you're about to grieve the Holy Spirit within you. God will guide our words and protect us from a whole heap of drama.

2. **Don't drag others into the mud.** This means we consider the preciousness of the relationships around us, including the person we're hoping will see that vague post we wrote. In the same way that we don't need unnecessary drama, our friends don't need it either. Drama is really just a mud pit, and if we care about our

friends, we'll steer them away from the pit, not into it. If you find yourself starting to relay a story about how someone wronged you, you're bringing unnecessary drama into the listener's life by dragging them into the mud with you. Think before you speak! Remember, friends don't invite friends into drama.

Friends don't invite friends into drama.

3. **Stop trespassing.** This sounds simple, but when you're prone to emotional trespassing (in other words, injecting yourself into a situation you have *no business in*), you invite drama into your peace. So, when you see one of those vague posts, don't reply. Don't add fuel to the fire. Or if you feel the need to reply, do it privately. This is something we need to get right for ourselves and our children. On many occasions, Jay and I have asked our teens (especially the younger ones) to take things off social media. We have a "take it down and ask why afterward" approach, because more often than not, kids don't even realize they're trespassing. They need to know that inviting drama over for dinner is a disaster waiting to happen.

4. **Stop, drop, and roll.** Think back to elementary school. Do you remember the slogan "Stop, drop, and roll"? I learned this simple saying when I was very young as a way to remember what to do in the case of a house fire.

The next time you're tempted to invite drama into your life, try this: "Stop, drop it, and roll on outta there." Do you need to be involved in the conversation? (Stop.) Are you bringing up past hurts and dragging people down? (Drop it.) Does the environment you're in encourage drama and strife? (Roll on outta there.)

5. **Don't stir things up.** Proverbs 15:1 says, "A gentle answer turns away wrath, but a harsh word stirs up anger" (NIV). Boy, ain't *that* the truth. Let me just add that a vague word stirs up anger too. If you feel the need to be vague because you're upset with someone, you probably shouldn't be talking about it at all. And putting things like "I can't believe some people" on Facebook—well, that's not getting us anywhere either.

The next time you're tempted to jump into drama online or in real life, ask yourself, *How is my presence in this situation going to help? Is it going to add unnecessary stress to my life or to someone else's?* If you can't justify your participation, walk away.

MOM**STRONG** MOM, SAY NO TO DRAMA

The bottom line: it's time to say no to drama, mama. If you need to address something that should be handled in private, then do it privately. If you've been hurt, don't put it on the Internet. Just say no to "vague-booking." Season your speech with grace. And if you're in a relationship that continually pulls you down into the mud, it might be time to consider putting up healthy boundaries on that relationship (and maybe even ending it).

While we'll never be totally drama-free this side of heaven, we can eliminate a lot of unnecessary conflict by being intentional about our relationships and the way we respond to divisive behavior. As mothers, we have an opportunity to show our children how to reduce drama in their lives as we do so in our own.

It's time to pursue peace—for our own sakes and for the sake of everyone who's watching. Because when we choose our battles according to God's leading instead of our flesh, it's a win-win every time.

I'm committing to being a "no-drama mama." How about you?

PRAYER POINTS FOR A
DRAMA-FREE MOM

- Pray that God will help you hear His voice when you're tempted to engage in gossip, whether online or in person (see Proverbs 16:28).
- Pray that your relationships will build others up, not tear them down (see Proverbs 14:1).
- Pray that God will guard you and your children against people with divisive spirits (see Titus 3:10).

Chapter 10

BIG GIRLS DO CRY

*I*t was raining the day a dear friend asked me to meet her at a coffee shop near my house. I thought we were meeting to catch up. After all, it had been a while since we'd had a conversation that wasn't just in passing. I was wrong.

As it turned out, my friend was angry with me. Her complaint threw me off kilter—I hadn't seen it coming at all. In fact, I had no idea she was harboring ill feelings toward me until she abruptly ended our friendship over a chai latte with extra cream.

Granted, there are two sides to every story. I'm sure that if she were writing this, she'd offer a different perspective. She was carrying a hurt I wasn't aware of. It's possible that I was so wrapped up in my busy life that I missed the signs of an unraveling relationship. Regardless, I felt blindsided and devastated.

Over the next several weeks, we tried to resolve the issue, but it wasn't getting better. Since we were unable to reconcile on our own, we asked another couple to sit in with us and mediate. I felt helpless as my husband and I sat with my friend and her husband in an attempt to follow Jesus' teachings in Matthew 18:15-20. The mediators tried to make progress. After a couple of hours of getting nowhere, we ended our meeting in prayer. Tears ran down my face and fell onto my lap. There was no fixing it. After years of friendship and a shared vision, it was all over. And there was nothing I could do to stop it.

Afterward, Jay and I walked quietly to our car in the church parking lot. Seeing the anguish in my eyes, he said gently, "We tried, Heidi. Sometimes you just need to walk away. Sometimes we can't understand. Sometimes the fight is worth it, and sometimes it isn't." He opened the car door for me, and I got in without saying a word.

We never met with our friends again.

In the weeks and months that followed, I tried to make sense of what felt to me like a net loss for the Kingdom. Two people we loved were struggling with something we couldn't understand—to the point that we could no longer be friends. It was heartbreaking for our entire family. I felt misunderstood and lonely. The stress of the fractured friendship took a toll on my peace and threatened to unravel my fragile self-confidence. Every time I saw my now former friend at an event in the community, my confidence took a hit. I wanted to cry and run away.

The blunt-force trauma that this experience inflicted on my inner person took me by surprise. I'm a fighter. I don't give up easily. And this idea of walking away was foreign to me. Surely there was *something I could do*—something that would bridge the gap and smooth the way. But as weeks turned to months and months turned to years, I realized there was nothing I could do. I wanted to be *understood*, but instead I'd been rejected.

Rejection is an emotion unlike any other. There's something visceral about this kind of pain. Even though my husband and I prayed that God would mend the friendship, for whatever reason, healing never came. The painful reality was this: sometimes walking away is the only thing you can do.

The lessons I learned in this season will stay with me forever. As with all hard things, either you learn from them or you don't. We are relational beings. We were created by God for relationship, first with Him and then with others. Fortunately, our relationship with God is 100 percent secure. He never changes; His love is unconditional and constant. There's nothing we can do that will make Him love us any more or any less. He doesn't give up on us.

We were created for relationship, first with God and then with others.

People aren't like that. People change. As a result, sometimes friendships can hurt. And boy, was I hurting. I began to ask the Lord to pull me up out of the pit I was in. Our children were junior high age and younger at the time. As part of our homeschooling program, we were reading through a children's

Bible together. One day, as we were reading about David and his many struggles, it occurred to me that David had overcome most of his pain and struggles by learning to allow God to fight on his behalf. There I was, trying to defend myself, agonizing over feelings of being misunderstood and rejected, and all the while God was saying, *Be still. I am your defender. Let Me speak for you.*

It took a while for me to understand, but in that season, being still meant walking away completely. In order to be still, I made the decision to block these friends on social media, because the temptation to see their family photos and find out what they were doing was only inviting more drama and stress into my life. Walking away meant not thinking about it anymore. It meant that I needed to stop trying to figure it out. It meant not giving rent-free space in my heart and mind to a situation that was beyond my control.

Don't give rent-free space in your heart and mind to a situation that's beyond your control.

In the end, I had to learn to trust God with a situation that I simply could not understand. As I've said before, the way we respond to trials puts our beliefs about God on display for everyone—especially our children—to see. Our kids saw us hurting, and we wanted them to see that we trusted God for healing, too.

Some mothers don't want their children to ever see them hurting, thinking this diminishes their strength somehow. I disagree with this philosophy because it's inconsistent with the role of a mother. We need to teach our children how to handle the ups and downs life throws at us. Our kids need to see that we don't value drama or the negativity that comes with it. They need to see us strive for peace in our homes and in our relationships.

MomStrong moms trust God to help them model healing for their children—even if it means their kids see them cry.

When all this was happening with our friends, some of our kids were old enough to understand what was going on. After all, the couple who was no longer in our lives was also no longer in our children's lives. Jay and I decided to talk to them about the situation, and in doing so, they became part of the healing God eventually brought to our family. Did they cry too? Yes. But we wanted them to know that God could be trusted and that sometimes you need to cry.

No matter how much we try to protect them, at some point our kids are going to face rejection. When we face it ourselves, it can be an opportunity to teach our children healthy ways to handle the emotions that follow. MomStrong moms trust God to help them model healing for their children—even if it means their kids see them cry.

JESUS UNDERSTANDS SUFFERING

A few years ago, musical artist Amy Grant wrote a beautiful song called "Better Than a Hallelujah." I can't tell you how many times I've listened to her song with tears in my eyes. My hunch is that Amy, like many of us moms, understands the beauty of brokenness.

> *Beautiful, the mess we are,*
> *The honest cries of breaking hearts*
> *Are better than a hallelujah.*

God doesn't expect us to be happy all the time. He understands that we aren't always in a hallelujah place in our lives. He loves us and accepts us right where we are. And what's more, the Bible teaches that He's actually *closer* to us when we're struggling and suffering than at any other time in life. The Bible says, "The Lord is close to the brokenhearted; he rescues those whose spirits are crushed"(Psalm 34:18). It's when we're suffering that we experience God's peace more acutely than at any other time.

God is close to the brokenhearted. He's near to the woman who has been abused and abandoned. He understands the indescribable pain of a woman facing rejection. He longs to comfort the mom who has lost a child, born or unborn. God sees the woman struggling with the sting of regret over choices she has made. He sees the mother who sits alone on her bedroom floor at night, eyes wet with tears, clutching a picture of her broken family in her hands. He longs to touch and comfort us. *He understands.*

Of all the characteristics I love about my God, the one that touches me most is that He has made me in His image. If we are emotional beings, we'd better believe that God is also emotional. God grieves too. He isn't aloof, indifferent, or unaware when His children are grieving. Instead, He is present in our suffering. He understands it because He, too, has suffered.

> *God isn't aloof, indifferent, or unaware when His children are grieving. He understands it because He, too, has suffered.*

"Jesus was so obviously *human*," notes Eugene Peterson.[1] He later says, "But this has never been an easy truth for people to swallow. There are always plenty of people around who will have none of this particularity; human ordinariness, bodily fluids, raw emotions of anger and disgust, fatigue and loneliness."[2]

The Gospels are filled with beautiful stories of the humanity of Jesus:

- He suffered (see Mark 8:31).
- He was hungry (see Luke 4:2).
- He was thirsty (see John 19:28).
- He was rejected (see Mark 12:10-12).
- He was beaten (see Mark 14:65).
- He was lonely (see Matthew 27:46).
- He was acquainted with grief.

Listen to what Isaiah says:

He was despised and rejected—
    a man of sorrows, acquainted with deepest grief.
We turned our backs on him and looked the other way.
    He was despised, and we did not care.

ISAIAH 53:3

Did you catch that last part? We didn't care. We looked the other way. We rejected Him. But still He doesn't reject us. God doesn't look the other way when He sees our suffering. Surely He has borne our sorrows. Surely He understands because He, too, has been broken.

One of the most emotional scenes in the Bible is found in John 11. It's the story of a man named Lazarus, the brother of Mary and Martha. It was Mary who anointed the Lord with oil and wiped His feet with her hair (see John 12:1-3). Jesus knew how much she loved Him, and He knew how much Lazarus meant to her. When Lazarus became gravely ill, the sisters sent a message asking Jesus to come, and yet Jesus waited two extra days before coming. Why? The answer is found in John 11:4. When Jesus heard Lazarus was ill, He said, "Lazarus's sickness will not end in death. No, it happened for the glory of God so that the Son of God will receive glory from this."

Not because He didn't care. Not because He was helpless to do anything. Not because He was ignoring their request. *So that the Son of God will receive glory.*

In 2 Corinthians 12:10, Paul says, "That's why I take pleasure in my weaknesses, and in the insults, hardships, persecutions, and troubles that I suffer for Christ." There's a reason we can and should "take pleasure" when we face a trial. We're facing these hardships so our lives can be living testimonies to the authentic healing and grace of God.

JESUS WEPT

As mothers, we need to understand—no, we need to *believe*—that God is always at work in our struggles, in part because we're teaching our children that God has a purpose in all things. Everything God does has a divine justification behind it, greater than we can know or understand this side of heaven. Yes, there is suffering in the world, but that isn't because God doesn't love us. Suffering is a result of sin, and it breaks the heart of the Father.

Just a little later in the story of Lazarus, the Bible says, "Now Jesus loved Martha and her sister and Lazarus" (John 11:5, NIV). Jesus saw the pain Mary and Martha were feeling. Notice the tender way Jesus responded to their pain: "When Jesus saw her weeping, and the Jews who had come along with her also weeping, he was deeply moved in spirit and troubled. 'Where have you laid him?' he asked" (John 11:33-34, NIV).

When Jesus was taken to the tomb, something remarkable happened: "Jesus wept" (John 11:35).

Jesus wept. Is there a more authentic human reaction than that? God knows firsthand the emotions we experience in this life. When Jesus saw Mary weeping, it grieved and upset Him.

I often wonder what Jesus was going through in that moment. Why did He weep? Some scholars say He wept over the suffering that sin brought into the perfect, beautiful world God had made. Some say it was because He wanted to be with the Father. Others claim that Jesus knew that in bringing Lazarus back to life, He would also be taking him away from the presence of

God. Who would want to come back to this broken place after experiencing the joy of heaven? However, I'm not sure any of those theories captures the full picture. I imagine Jesus was sorrowing in much the same way we grieve over the injustices of this fallen, broken world. After all, He is present in our broken world, and He feels the pain we feel.

Jesus understands how it feels to be brokenhearted. He knows what it's like to grieve over a wayward child, and He knows the pain of physical suffering. In the process of dying for our sin, He brought hope into our world. He wants us to depend on Him for everything—from the air we breathe to the relationships we're in.

Jesus offers respite from suffering and encouragement in the midst of it. He cares deeply about our suffering. In Psalm 56:8, David says, "You keep track of all my sorrows. You have collected all my tears in your bottle. You have recorded each one in your book." Can you imagine? God collects our tears and saves them. Not a single tear falls from our eyes that He isn't intimately familiar with—and it's all because of love.

Not a single tear falls from our eyes that God isn't intimately familiar with.

This may sound counterintuitive at first, but grief is evidence of love. The more you love, the more you grieve. But the good news is that God doesn't leave us alone in our grief. In a beautiful exchange, Jesus offers His grace for our sorrows, His peace for our pain, and His hope for our fears. There's grace in abundance for the brokenhearted mom at the feet of Jesus Christ. He offers healing from the past and hope for the future. It's all there—we need only ask.

The idea of being dependent on God doesn't sit well with many of us who were raised to be independent, liberated, self-reliant, self-made women. We're taught to be in control. Our culture rewards the strong and discards the weak. But God doesn't operate according to the world's values. Instead, He offers strength to the weak and healing to the broken. He understands our suffering, and He offers a special blessing to those who find themselves in pain:

> God blesses those who mourn, for they will be comforted.
> MATTHEW 5:4

Precious mom, we are broken people living in a broken, sin-filled world. But we serve a God who promises to help us.

> I hold you by your right hand—
>   I, the LORD your God.
> And I say to you,
>   "Don't be afraid. I am here to help you."
> ISAIAH 41:13

I cling to this hope—not only for myself, but also for my children. I know I can't always prevent my children from experiencing the pain they're sure to encounter in this life, but I can lead them to the One who has borne their sorrows and who collects their tears.

WHEN THERE ARE NO WORDS

There's nothing quite like seeing those positive lines on a pregnancy test. Only a mother knows what it's like to bond with an unborn baby. We dream of little fingers and toes. We make room in our hearts and in our homes. When the pregnancy is confirmed, so is the bond. And it lasts forever.

In 2000, I became pregnant with our fourth child. We were thrilled, but we decided to wait a few weeks before making an official announcement. Jay and I have never been very good at keeping pregnancies a secret for very long, and after sharing a few days of quiet joy between the two of us, we told our children and close family.

Everyone knows that once the kids hear the news, it's best to just shout it out loud to the rest of the world, and that's exactly what we did. The next day we made an announcement to Jay's ministry team and pastoral staff, and word spread quickly.

Not too long after the announcement, I went in for a routine doctor's appointment. When no heartbeat could be detected, I went down the hall for an ultrasound, which confirmed my worst fear: we had lost our baby.

Since I'd been expecting a short, routine visit, Jay wasn't with me. Worse yet, the technician was a student, and her interpretation of my ultrasound came off as clinical and uncaring. Alone in the exam room, I was told it appeared our baby had died just a few days earlier. I could expect to start bleeding within a few days. Then the technician gave me instructions to follow in the event that I didn't start bleeding: "Just come back, and we'll perform a D and C."

In that moment, my heart was broken. I got up off the table and numbly put my clothes back on. After I left the office,

I went to see Jay, and we grieved together—not only for the loss of our sweet baby but for the loss of our dreams of what our family might have looked like after his or her arrival. We grieved about the fact that I'd been at the doctor's office alone, about the callousness of the ultrasound technician, and about the clinical response to my obvious shock and pain.

Later that week, Jay announced to the choir and ministry team that we'd lost our baby. Here are just a few of the things we heard from well-meaning but misguided friends and family in the days that followed:

"At least you can have another baby."

"At least you didn't get further along!"

"This is God's way of sparing you from the pain of a disabled child."

"You'll get over it."

Can we just agree that we're not very good at comforting someone who has experienced a loss? These awful comments didn't come from awful people, but they hurt nonetheless. Yet even in my pain, I understood the awkward roots of these statements. In fact, I'm sure that on more than one occasion I've inadvertently said something to someone in pain that came across as unfeeling and cold. Sometimes even well-meaning people say things that wound others.

I learned a couple of painful lessons from the loss of our baby—chief among them that I don't ever want to be in a hurry to fix someone else's pain. It's difficult to know what to say when someone is grieving, and we often try to fill the empty space with words. The words are meant to bring a positive out of a negative, but all they do is downplay the legitimate pain that person is experiencing.

In reality, the person who is suffering doesn't need our words. They just need our presence. It's enough to be there when a person you know is struggling. Dropping by with a cup of hot coffee or a bouquet of flowers will speak volumes. Sometimes pain is too deep for words.

If you're going through the grieving process right now or if you know someone who is, be comforted. God's timetable for grief is His alone. You can't rush the grieving process, because we never really "get over" grief. We just get through it.

And rest assured, precious mom, you will get through it.

HELPING OUR CHILDREN PROCESS THEIR EMOTIONS

"Stop crying!"

I have no idea how many times I heard this as a child, but it was enough to make me feel ashamed of my tears. By the time I was seventeen, I had learned to stuff my emotions. I was so rehearsed in the art of making excuses that I lived with a constant stomachache. In my early twenties, I was diagnosed with my first stomach ulcer. I learned the hard way that when you swallow negative emotions, your body gets sick.

Moms, don't teach your children to swallow their emotions. Feelings are just that: feelings. They're neither right nor wrong. When we ignore our children's struggles or minimize them, we're setting our children up for a lifetime of difficulty processing their emotions.

Wise moms teach their children to handle their emotions, even the unwieldy ones. And we can't do that if we don't let our children express their feelings. Of course, there are right ways and wrong ways to express emotions. But when we don't let our children talk about their feelings, chances are they'll end up taking their negative emotions out on others.

David knew better than anyone what happens when we bottle up our pain. In Psalm 32:3, David writes, "When I kept things to myself, I felt weak deep inside me. I moaned all day long" (NCV). In this passage, David is referring to an unconfessed sin that was troubling him. The point remains the same, whether we need to make a confession or share a struggle: bottling our feelings inside is not the answer.

We weren't made to go it alone when dealing with emotions. As you grow as a mother and as a daughter of God, take confidence in this truth: you can cry out to God.

GRIEVING THROUGH SEASONS OF CHANGE

Motherhood is an ever-changing, soul-altering thing. One minute you're mothering a helpless infant, and the next that "infant" is ready to fly the comfortable nest you've spent a couple of decades feathering. Change can be hard on a mother's heart, but without it, we don't grow.

When our youngest was two years old, I had a hysterectomy and became a grandmother in the space of six weeks. A few days before my hysterectomy, as I was doing laundry, a blanket caught my eye. It boasted a Daisy Kingdom pattern from the nineties. I loved that blanket—I'd stitched it together in my kitchen while I waited for my first baby to arrive. It had graced the cribs of all seven of my children, and now it was time for it to grace a new crib. Time was moving forward.

I went downstairs and put the blanket in a box of things I was getting ready to give to my oldest daughter. The blanket was hers, really. My heart ached for how quickly those past twenty-two years had gone by. Other moms had told me they would go by fast, but I hadn't believed them.

As I went through the house that night, I thought of other things I wouldn't need anymore—things I'd been holding on to "just in case." A newborn car seat cover. A handful of handmade burp cloths. A breast pump. Nursing covers. I took them downstairs and placed them in the box next to the blanket.

It felt like a surrender of sorts.

As I continued to clean, I glanced up in my closet and saw bins of baby clothes. I noticed a little green coat that baby number seven had outgrown too quickly. I had asked her to wear it long after the sleeves were too short, long after it should have been surrendered to storage. I knew it was time to move on, but as the tears ran down my face, I realized that for all my bravado about how glad I was to be done with diapers, I was going to miss this stage.

This is silly, I thought. *Look at those bins, just taking up space in my closet.* And in my heart. As I took the bins down from the closet shelf, the memories came flooding back.

Newborn.
Up all night.
The sound of little feet.
Doing math lessons.
(Forgetting I was) the tooth fairy.
Watching grasshoppers.
Catching crickets.
Giving driving lessons.
Graduation.

Going to college.
Married.
Moving on.
New life.
And it starts again.

They grow so quickly, don't they?

It's impossible to grasp the brevity of life. The days go by so slowly, yet the years go by so fast. I wonder . . . if we knew how fast the time would go, would we stop longer, linger more, savor more? I think we would.

The world may see motherhood as little more than a stopover on the highway of life, but I want to see *so much more*. I want to soak up the seasons of my life in such a way that it pains me to see them pass. MomStrong moms savor the moments and the days and the years. Yes, there is pain in the changes. But something tells me that if it hurts, we're doing it right.

MOM**STRONG** MOM, HAVE HOPE

One of my favorite verses in the Bible is Jeremiah 29:11: "'I know the plans I have for you,' says the LORD. 'They are plans for good and not for disaster, to give you a future and a hope.'"

A future and a hope. God knew we would need both! And yet how quickly we forget His promises. That's why He sent the Holy Spirit, the Comforter, to us—to remind us of the hope we have in Him.

Of all the emotions we have as women, hope is the one that shows God's heart most clearly. Hope bubbles to the surface of our souls with the tiniest word of encouragement; it shoots to the top of our other emotions with the faintest reminder from God's Word: "all things work together for [our] good" (Romans 8:28, KJV). Hope that is based on faith in Jesus Christ floats—even in the midst of an ocean of grief and suffering—because when we place our hope in Him alone, our hope is never misplaced.

Though we suffer loss and rejection, we don't grieve like the world grieves. We grieve with hope: "Dear brothers and sisters, we want you to know what will happen to the believers who have died so you will not grieve like people who have no hope" (1 Thessalonians 4:13).

Our hope is this: one day God is going to settle the score. One day God will wipe away every tear from our eyes. One day God will make all things new. When I read my Bible, I am reminded that this life isn't all there is! Hallelujah! Our hope is found in Jesus, and because of Him, we have a wonderful eternity to look forward to: "No eye has seen, no ear has heard, and no mind has imagined what God has prepared for those who love him" (1 Corinthians 2:9).

Are you brokenhearted, precious mom? Take heart: God is near.

PRAYER POINTS FOR A
GRIEVING MOM

- Pray that you will have the courage to process your pain and bring it to God instead of bottling it up inside (see Psalm 32:3).
- Pray that you will be able to encourage others who are struggling, simply by being present (see Job 2:13).
- Pray that you will be able to help your children understand and talk about the difficult emotions they experience (see Proverbs 15:13).

Chapter 11

RELAX—
GOD'S GOT THIS!

*O*kay. Time to take a deep breath. Literally. I know you have a million things to do today (what mom doesn't?), but this is important. Trust me. I know what I'm talking about—well, at least now I do. Sadly, that hasn't always been the case.

Six years ago, when my blog was starting to take off and I was accepting more speaking opportunities, I realized something. No—that's not entirely true. It was more like my kids called a meeting. They elected a representative to make their first appeal. Savannah approached me as I was working in the kitchen. "Mom? Can we talk? Would you like some tea?"

I hesitated.

"Can you sit down for a minute?" she continued. "The kids sent me to talk to you."

Uh-oh. This could not be good.

"We've been talking, and here's the thing, Mom. You know the Egyptian sarcophagus that we started making last year for world history? Well, we never finished it. And remember that time you said we were going to go on a walk every day and pretend we were explorers like Lewis and Clark? Well, we only went for two walks. And remember . . . ?" This went on for what felt like forever before she finally concluded, "We don't think you're fun anymore."

In an instant, everything I'd promised God I would work on with my kids—patience, maturity, good listening—was forgotten. I was mad and hurt. I felt like giving up, but instead I just lashed out.

"Oh really?" I said. "Well, right back at you! I don't think you're much fun either! When was the last time you offered to help me clean up the sarcophagus mess without being asked? Huh? That's why I quit! And I didn't like taking walks every day since all you kids did was argue about who found what first! So I guess it goes both ways, doesn't it?"

Savannah looked at the floor, avoiding my icy stare. "Well, I guess I'll tell the kids." And with that, she got up quietly and left me alone with a baby on my lap and a badly bruised ego. I suppose a good mom would have gone after her and apologized, but I was just so tired. And I confess—I was embarrassed, too. Kids see the real us, don't they?

In my effort to make everyone happy, it seemed I wasn't making anyone happy. Including myself. I was struggling to keep up with daily life. I was easily irritated. Things that used to bring me joy no longer did. I needed to hit the reset button.

When Jay came home from work, he found me pouting in

our bedroom. The kids had been watching reruns of Veggie-Tales all day. After Jay spent an hour talking me down from my emotional tree, we decided it would be good to have a family sit-down, so after dinner, we all gathered in the living room. One by one the four oldest kids expressed how they'd been feeling. They pointed out that one of our favorite family pastimes, reading aloud together, was no longer enjoyable. The four-year-old observed that I read everything at warp speed, and apparently my voice sounded "angry." Ouch. That wasn't exactly the mom I wanted them to remember—more like the mom I hoped they'd forget.

After talking with the kids, my husband and I realized we had to make a couple of big decisions regarding our priorities. I didn't want motherhood to be an afterthought, but the truth was clear: if something didn't change, that's exactly what it was going to be. There was no way I could manage all that was on my plate and still be the wife and mother I wrote about on my blog.

Jay and I began to pray about the situation, asking God for wisdom beyond our experience. After several weeks of prayerful consideration, we made the decision to rearrange our lives so that our investment of time and energy would better reflect the things we truly cared about. I backed off, deciding to stop handling all the technical aspects of my blog, and Jay stepped up, taking a more active role in helping me with things like after-dinner cleanup and weekend work. In a huge leap of faith, we took what little income my blog was generating and hired a part-time assistant to help, freeing my time to be where my heart was: with our children.

It took a little time, but before long, reading aloud was a

joyful, wonderful experience again. As it turns out, moms can't do it all. And that's okay.

As it turns out, moms can't do it all. And that's okay.

WHAT NEEDS TO COME OFF YOUR PLATE?

I know it's tempting to think we can do it all. But in the past twenty years, I've met many gifted moms—bloggers, authors, organic gardeners, homeschool superstars, speakers, nurses, doctors, attorneys, and foster moms—and guess what? I've never met one, myself included, who can do it all. Sometimes you just have to let go and trust that God has everything under control. If I were sitting with you right now, I'd look you right in your beautiful mama-eyes and remind you that you can trust God. He has a plan, and I promise, it doesn't include burning you out and leaving your family resentful and sad.

If we're going to be strong as mothers, we have to start being honest about where we invest our time and energy. Brutally honest. The increasing use of antianxiety medication in our culture is telling. It seems that despite all the advantages modern technology affords us, we're a generation of stressed-out mothers.

As a recovering control freak, I'm here to tell you something: most of the stress in our lives comes because we put it there. (Don't get mad at me!) Let's think this through for a moment.

Sure, there are things that happen that are outside our control. Children get sick. Jobs end. For the most part, the truly bad things that happen to us are unplanned and largely unpreventable. Am I suggesting that we stop buckling our kids into their car seats because we can't control our futures? Absolutely not. Do what you can—and then live your life in such a way that your children can see where your trust is.

When we live our lives in a pressure cooker of our own design, what we're saying to our children is that we don't believe God is capable of handling the problems and struggles life throws at us. When we believe God is in control of our circumstances, we free ourselves to move from stress into a position of strength. It all comes back to priorities.

God has a plan, and it doesn't include burning you out and leaving your family resentful and sad.

So what's on your plate that shouldn't be there? What can you remove or hand off to someone else? What outside activities have you committed to that aren't yielding the return you hoped they would? What have you said yes to without first seeking the Lord? Are your children and husband getting the rest of you . . . or the best of you?

Tired mom, think with me for a minute. How many times are we "too busy" to pray and access the divine power God wants to give us? How many times have we denied our souls the chance to drink from living water in favor of something else? If we're honest, this is all too easy to do. It's easy to become busy and forget that the job of mothering this generation has made us a target for the enemy of our souls.

Listen: Satan is a lot of things, but he's no dummy. He knows that a weary, worn-out mom is going to be less likely to pray and read her Bible—and this is often where the cycle of fear and weakness begins. For example, have you ever felt the sting that comes from letting your flesh dictate your response to a mouthy child? I have! Oh, how I've regretted things I've spoken out of a weary, dry soul. When we allow ourselves to believe the lie that we can do this mothering thing apart from the grace of God, weariness starts to settle into the deep places of our hearts.

> *When we allow ourselves to believe the lie that we can do this mothering thing apart from the grace of God, weariness starts to settle into the deep places of our hearts.*

When I'm frustrated or tired, my human response to stress is often to phone a friend or find counsel from a good book or a speaker. Meanwhile, God is saying, *I'm here! Come to Me, and I will give your battle-worn heart a rest. Let Me restore you.*

The next time life throws you a curveball, stop and pray. Pray with your kids. Pray in the quiet of your own heart. Ask God to cover you, and then live like a woman who believes she is protected and loved. Remember, you're a daughter of the King, and He wants to spend time with you. Taking just a few minutes each day to read the Bible and lay your burdens at His feet will make all the difference in the world.

WANNA WRESTLE?

As you know, I have seven children. The oldest is now twenty-six, and our youngest is six. (Yes, that's a twenty-year age span. Keep moving. Nothing to see here.) When my oldest child turned one, I had a "Pinterest" board in my head for what a first birthday party should look like—even though the Internet hadn't even been born yet. And because I was young and naive and had a lot more time on my hands, my first child's first birthday party was an extravaganza fit for a princess. By the time our seventh child turned one, however—between juggling a toddler, a daughter who wanted to get married, two teens, two kids in elementary school, and a kindergartner—the very thought of making a cake from scratch gave me hives.

In fact, let me break it down for you:

First Child's First Birthday

Birthday cake made from scratch. It rocked, and she didn't know it.

Handwritten invitations were sent to everyone we knew.

Scrapbooked every little move (at least one hundred pictures).

Promptly sent thank-you cards to guests.

Second Child's First Birthday

I made her cake too—a little less extravagant, but lovely.
Sent handwritten postcards to a few moms I knew.
Scrapbooked most of the highlights (probably twenty-five
    pictures).
Got thank-you notes sent within two months.

Third Child's First Birthday

Store-bought cake. Lucky, since he was the first boy.
Called the grandparents to see if they wanted to join us.
Staged a photo shoot. (We only needed five pictures.)
No invitations were sent, and I thanked the grandparents
    on site.

Fourth Child's First Birthday

Skipped it. By this time, I knew he wouldn't appreciate it,
    and I was too tired.

Fifth Child's First Birthday

A celebration of the fourth and the fifth children at once.
Invited a few other tired moms to meet me at Chuck E.
    Cheese's so the big kids would have something to do.
All moms present agreed to a no-thank-you-note policy.

Sixth Child's First Birthday

Can't remember it. No kidding. I hope she'll forgive me.

Seventh Child's First Birthday

Asked grandma to make a cake.
Put the five- and seven-year-olds on decorations.

Tried to keep the baby up long enough to get a picture. Birthday prayer was that I would have the strength to get all the younger kids in bed by seven thirty.

Whether you have one kid or a dozen, it's a marathon— this thing we call motherhood. Just as beginning a marathon requires courage and determination, finishing one requires endurance. By now you should know me well enough to realize that I'm going to point your weary, overachieving heart back to the Word of God. (Note that I'm preaching to myself here too, as usual!) As it turns out, God's wisdom is for tired moms. Why? Because we are God's creations, and He knows us better than we know ourselves. In fact, God knows the hearts of tired mothers intimately because He works the night shift with us.

> *God knows the hearts of tired mothers intimately because He works the night shift with us.*

Maybe, like me, you struggle to rest. I've come to call this w*rest*ling. See if you see yourself in my struggle-to-rest test:

- I wrestle to give myself permission to slow down, even when I know I need to.
- I wrestle with the fear that resting will cause me to fall behind, even though the opposite is true.
- I wrestle with the lie that resting equals weakness.

- I wrestle to make time in my life for rest.
- I wrestle to acknowledge my need for rest.
- I wrestle with the truth that rest is necessary for me to be the mom I want to be.

Like any worthy goal, rest must be seen as a necessary discipline if we're going to do all that's before us with joy. Jesus said that rest is essential to life: "Come to me, all of you who are weary and carry heavy burdens, and I will give you rest. Take my yoke upon you. Let me teach you, because I am humble and gentle at heart, and you will find rest for your souls" (Matthew 11:28-29).

Jesus is giving three imperatives in this well-known passage of Scripture. The first is simple, but it's something we struggle with in our culture of go, go, go: "Come to me." Rest is found when we focus our eyes on God. He is the *source* of rest. Apart from Him, we can do nothing (see John 15:5).

When I was a child, the words to the hymn "Turn Your Eyes upon Jesus" became etched on my heart. Grandma sang it to me many nights as she tucked me into bed under starched white sheets and the weight of my mother's childhood quilt.

Turn your eyes upon Jesus,
Look full in His wonderful face,
And the things of earth will grow strangely dim,
In the light of His glory and grace.

The old hymn is right: the world must grow dim if we're going to find rest in Him. It isn't easy to tune out things like social media, phone calls, and texts. It isn't easy to say no to volunteering for just one more committee at church or in the community. It isn't easy to give yourself permission to tell your adult children that you need a day off—even from your grandchildren. But it's necessary if we're going to stay in this motherhood thing long-term.

So how can we stop wrestling and start resting? We can begin by treating rest as we would any other important commitment or task. (Oh man, am I ever preaching to myself right now!) Ask the Lord for the discipline to turn off any unnecessary distractions. Get alone with God, and then turn your eyes upon Jesus. He promises to give us rest and to refresh us in a way only He can.

I've said this before, and I'll say it again: spending time with the Lord is nonnegotiable if you want to become the mother God created you to be. You have to make time for God, not excuses.

The second imperative Jesus gives in this passage is one that we often overlook, especially those of us who are addicted to saying yes: "Take my yoke upon you." The imagery here is so powerful! I didn't grow up on a working farm, but I did watch the entire *Little House on the Prairie* series, so I'm practically an expert. Pa sure knew how to drive that plow, and when the oxen were yoked together, they worked in harmony. One made the other's load easier.

Imagine the God of the universe looking at you and offering to take the other half of the yoke you're pulling. That's what God wants to do! When we're yoked with God, all things are possible. Stop and think with me for a moment: Are you wearing His yoke? Or are you wearing one of your own design? One thing is for sure: when I wear a yoke of my choosing, it's not easy or light. It's burdensome and heavy—the opposite of the yoke Jesus offers.

So in practical terms, what does it mean to take up the yoke of Christ? It means listening to God for direction. When we take His yoke, we're taking only the assignments He gives us. Nothing more, nothing less. His yoke, His timing.

Then there's the third and final imperative: "Let me teach you." Don't you love the gentle instruction of the Good Shepherd here? I can almost picture God shaking His head at me right after I said yes to that thing I should have said no to. *No, Heidi, no. This way. Learn from Me.*

In order to learn from Jesus, we have to be in His Word. Learning from Jesus requires prayer and quiet reflection—unless you're a mom with little ones. I believe mothers of little ones have a special grace over them. I call it "quiet grace," because it allows us to sit at the feet of Jesus even in the midst of a noisy household.

Becoming MomStrong means that we become students of the Lord. Mothers are also teachers, and when a mom learns from the Lord, so do her children. It sounds easier than it is, I know—especially in times of stress and struggle. Most of us aren't born with the ability to just chill out in the middle of stress. We need to learn.

If you're struggling right now, check out David's wise words in Psalm 62:

> Let all that I am wait quietly before God,
>   for my hope is in him.
> He alone is my rock and my salvation,
>   my fortress where I will not be shaken.
> My victory and honor come from God alone.

He is my refuge, a rock where no enemy can reach me.
O my people, trust in him at all times.
Pour out your heart to him,
for God is our refuge.

PSALM 62:5-8

If you've ever watched a brother or sister in Christ go through tremendous stress and heartache with true peace and wondered how, this is how. It's God's peace—the peace that comes from knowing He is our rock and our refuge. No matter what's happening around you, your soul can find rest and peace in God. He won't let you down.

MOM**STRONG** MOM, PACE YOURSELF

MomStrong moms recognize that the road is long. You don't need to sprint. Slow and steady will get you there just fine. So pace yourself, precious mom—you're in this for the marathon. "Run with endurance the race God has set before us" (Hebrews 12:1).

If you're struggling to give yourself permission to take a break, I understand. I'm almost allergic to just sitting around. Bear in mind, however, that resting doesn't just mean sleeping. It means taking a break from things that cause stress. Whatever it is that brings you joy—whatever refreshes you—that's rest. Maybe that's watching your favorite series on Netflix. Maybe it's crocheting or blogging or taking a bubble bath. Since we're all different, we all rest differently. And that's okay.

My point is, don't be afraid to do what you need to do to take care of yourself—body, mind, and spirit. You have an important job to do: raising the next generation of warriors. God needs you to be at your very best. So do your children. The veteran moms were right when they told me that the days are long but the years go by fast. So do yourself—and your children—a favor: slow down and enjoy them. (PS: no one will know if you use a cake mix. You're welcome.)

PRAYER POINTS FOR A
RESTFUL MOM

- Pray that God will show you what needs to come off your plate so you can say yes to the most important things (see Matthew 5:37).
- Pray that God will help you to rest in Him (see Matthew 11:28-29).
- Pray that God will enable you to model healthy rest for your children (see Hebrews 4:9).

Chapter 12

THE NEW NORMAL

"*I*'m just so tired all the time," I whined to my husband. "When are our lives going to go back to normal?" Sixteen years into parenting, and I was still wondering when I was going to get a full eight hours of sleep. (Spoiler alert—I'm still waiting.)

It seems as if this myth of "normal" has been around for a long time. But honestly, I'm not sure our lives ever return to normal after we have babies. It's been twenty-six years since I brought my first tiny miracle home from the hospital, and normal is still nowhere in sight.

Just like "wife" or "homeschooler," "tired" has become part of my identity, especially during particularly stressful or busy seasons of motherhood. For that matter, so has "absentminded." When I'm trying to juggle too many activities and/or people at once, I tend to forget things. For example, lately I've discovered that I need to write things like "drink water" on my to-do list. Otherwise, I forget. (Thank God breathing is pretty much automatic.)

As with all worthwhile opportunities in this life, motherhood comes with a cost. And if we're going to make it to the finish line, we need to figure out a way to stay focused and energized—especially during those busy seasons of nonstop feedings, diaper changes, carpooling, after-school activities, and the teenage years . . . including (deep breath) dating. We have to be strong. We have to be MomStrong.

Read on, tired mom. I promise you, relief is in sight. (Meanwhile, I'll keep asking Siri to remind me to drink more water. You might want to think about doing that too. You're welcome.)

EXHAUSTION IS THE DEVIL'S PLAYGROUND

Do you know what happens to sleep-deprived drivers? They get into accidents. The same rule applies to motherhood: tired moms are prime candidates for burnout. Have you ever been done? You know, *done*, as in "do your own laundry and find your own food" kind of done? Me, too. When I'm tired, here's what happens:

- I tend to avoid reading my Bible.
- My house turns into a 24/7 movie theater (aka "video babysitter").
- Homework doesn't get done.
- Laundry piles up.
- The slow cooker gets dusty.
- The kids don't get disciplined (just telling the truth here, people).

- School doesn't happen.
- I stop shaving my legs. And showering.

And I don't care. About any of it. When I'm close to burning out, I tend to check out. I'm guessing that if we were having a tall pumpkin spice latte together right now, you'd be high-fiving me. Why? Because we've all been there.

Here's the thing: the key word in burnout is *burn*. Burnout happens when we focus for too long on the wrong things, such as keeping up with the Joneses or saying yes when we should say no. We have to stay on top of these little flare-ups before they turn into full-blown brush fires. And it's not just our individual homes and families we need to be concerned about. Look around: the entire battlefield is ablaze right now. Our kids can't afford to have moms who are burned out and checked out. They need us to be all in.

Our kids can't afford to have moms who are burned out and checked out. They need us to be all in.

God has given this generation of moms a special challenge: to train future warriors for the spiritual battle that's unfolding around us. God is asking today's mothers to be strong in the midst of an incredibly powerful cultural shift away from the truth of God's Word.

It's an awesome responsibility, and in all honesty, it's daunting. Christian parents have the privilege and responsibility of teaching their children what it means to be strong in the Lord and in the power of His strength. The devil knows this. He knows that if the mothers of this generation are too exhausted to fight, they'll be tempted to give up. Tired parents have a tendency to look for ways to relieve the stress of parenting by relegating their sacred calling to pastors and teachers. Simply put, when the going gets tough, many moms are checking out.

MomStrong moms don't check out. They check in—all in. One hundred percent!

PRAY OR BE PREY

Being all in starts with a personal commitment to recognizing Jesus Christ as our source of strength. MomStrong moms need to prioritize their relationships with the living God in the same way they prioritize every other life-giving aspect of their lives. Think about it—just one day without water leads to dehydration. Well, our souls are no different. That's why we can't afford to go a single day without connecting with the Lord, either through His Word or in prayer. Doing so puts us at risk for spiritual dehydration.

One of my favorite verses is Isaiah 40:31: "Those who hope in the Lord will renew their strength. They will soar on wings like eagles; they will run and not grow weary, they will walk and not be faint" (NIV). Read that again. Now one more time. (It's okay—I'll wait. This is important.)

The prophet is pointing us to the source of all strength: the Lord! He's reminding us that it is the Lord who renews our strength. Do you want to run and not grow weary? Drink from the living water! We were born to thirst for our Creator. Without coming to Him daily, we'll eventually find ourselves weary, weak, and discouraged.

If we don't connect with the Lord, we're putting ourselves at risk for spiritual dehydration.

It's no wonder the enemy is working overtime to discourage and deplete moms. Think of it this way: a mom who is too tired to pray and read her Bible is no real threat to the devil. A tired mom is more likely to let the Internet parent her children. She's apt to miss the subtle signs of a child whose heart is far from the Lord. A tired mom is less likely to spend time with God, and without filling up at the source, she runs on empty.

Trust me, I've been there. You start motherhood fresh and energized. You have everything under control. You nap when baby naps. Friends bring you premade dinners so you don't have to cook. Your mother-in-law stops by to help with laundry. You schedule date nights with your spouse. You might even arrange a spa day for yourself every couple of weeks. After all, there's almost always a friend or a family member who can fill in for you for the afternoon. But then one kid turns into two (or three, or seven), and all of a sudden, you're in full-on mom mode.

In a blink, your life has become nothing but car pools and Crock-Pots from the moment you wake up until you lay your head down again at night. Date nights vanish. Sitters become harder (and more expensive) to find. Laundry piles up. And before you know it, you're eating leftover tuna casserole three days in a row and wondering when you last washed your own hair.

Let's face it: *busy* doesn't even begin to describe most moms today. We're often too distracted to ask God for help with our daily challenges. And Satan loves it when we're too busy to pray. Why? Because a mom who is too busy to seek the Lord in prayer is easy prey for the devil! Peter warns that our enemy is like a "roaring lion" (1 Peter 5:8). And this lion knows exactly how to get to the heart of a weary mom and drag her into the brush. But consider this, precious mom: in the midst of all the Crock-Pot meals, curriculum planning, and car pools, God wants to be your shelter. He wants to give you refuge from the chaos of the day.

> A mom who is too busy to seek the Lord in prayer is easy prey for the devil!

The psalmist offers a beautiful illustration of what it looks like to live under the covering of the Creator:

> He will cover you with his feathers.
> He will shelter you with his wings.
> His faithful promises are your armor and protection.
> PSALM 91:4

I love to imagine myself snuggled up under the feathers of my Lord Jesus, safely nestled under the wings of God Himself. What an awe-inspiring picture of the love and protection God offers His children! MomStrong moms depend on that protection. They access God's strength and power by coming to Him every day.

Try it, precious mom. Take a drink of living water every morning, and stay in tune with the Spirit throughout the day by praying and listening for that still, small voice. Yours is an awesome responsibility, so don't be afraid to go directly to the Lord when you need help. Share your challenges with Him, day and night, and let Him be your shelter. He is listening. He always will be.

THE ELEPHANT IN THE ROOM

In the fall of 2011, I was in a serious funk. The increasing demands of my personal and professional life were unraveling my resolve to be the wife and mom I wanted to be. I was exhausted and discouraged. I'd stopped exercising, because I couldn't find the time, and my libido was a negative three, meaning if my husband even looked at me "like that," I felt resentful. This was *not* who I wanted to be. So after a little wrestling with my pride, I made an appointment to see my doctor.

"Heidi," she said, after listening to me cry and complain for a while. "Do you know how to eat an elephant? Because it seems to me that you have an elephant to eat. You have seven kids. You work full-time. You're homeschooling. You have a vitamin deficiency. If that's not an elephant, I don't know what is."

Of course, she was right about all those things. I just needed an official diagnosis. You know. Just to be sure.

So how *do* you eat an elephant?

One. Bite. At. A. Time.

Yep. It was time for me to step back and look my elephant in his big ol' elephant eyes. Naturally, my elephant started as a baby elephant. He arrived on my doorstep with a cute little bow on his cute little head shortly after I made an unconscious decision: I stopped consulting the Lord about the commitments I was taking on outside my home.

Before I knew it, I was in over my head. My elephant was running faster and faster. I couldn't keep up. Little missteps were turning into big problems. I was overcommitted in almost every area of my life. I said yes when I should have said no, and I said no when I knew in my heart that I needed to say yes. And in the midst of it all, I forgot to take care of myself.

Can you relate? Are you tired of struggling to find balance and energy to meet the demands of everyday life? Well, breathe deeply with me, mom, and read on, because God cares about the way you take care of your body—and so should you.

Start Small

I love the smell of possibility in the morning. I love *being* up in the early morning. But I'll be honest: *getting* up is hard for me. Also, I'll confess that I don't like to exercise. I'm sorry—it's just not something I love to do. For many years my only "exercise routine" was chasing toddlers. And it worked—for a while. But in 2001, shortly after our fourth child was born, I ended up in the ER with excruciating back pain.

As we were sitting in the MRI suite, my husband looked at me and said, "Girl, you are held together with duct tape and baling wire!"

As it turned out, he was right. The scans showed I had several small fractures in my lower back. The doctor gave me two choices: surgery or exercise. Within a week, I came up with a plan. It was sketchy, but at least it was something. I decided to go to the gym three mornings a week. Unfortunately, the only time I could go was before my husband went to work, which—even more unfortunately—meant dragging my duct-taped body out of bed *very* early.

You know where this is going, don't you? That's right—after two weeks, I gave up. I simply wasn't in a season where it made sense for me to go to the gym. Shoot, I was lucky if I could sneak in even a five-minute shower every morning. Going to the gym? Forget about it!

Frustration set in. One morning I was discussing my disappointment with Jay, and he said something so simple, I almost didn't listen. "Do what you can," he said. "Start with something you know you can do. Get out and walk with the kids. Better to do something small than nothing at all."

It was sheer genius. (Some lucky girl really ought to marry that man!)

My commitment to getting physically stronger started with just ten minutes a day. I figured I could do almost anything for ten minutes. Eventually, those ten minutes turned into forty-five. Some days I have more time, so I do more. Other days, I might have only twenty minutes. Regardless, I make an effort to do something six mornings a week.

Here's a little window into my entirely-seasonal-but-hey-it's-working-for-me-today workout routine:

6:15–6:30 a.m.: Alarm goes off.
6:30–6:35 a.m.: Finally stop hitting snooze and check my
    phone for messages.

6:35–6:45 a.m.: Open my Bible app and read.

6:45–7:00 a.m.: Put on my workout clothes. (This is key, women!)

7:00–7:15 a.m.: Stretch.

7:15–7:40 a.m.: Get on my elliptical machine (which I bought for fifty dollars on Craigslist).

7:40–8:00 a.m.: Strength training, stretching.

You may be reading this and thinking that my little workout plan is wimpy. Sure, it's not exactly CrossFit or P90X, but it's working for me. Or you may be saying, "Are you kidding? I've only gotten three hours of sleep by 6:15 a.m.!"

That's okay. You don't have to go from zero to hero overnight. Just commit to doing *something*. Stop looking at exercise as something else you need to make time for, and start looking for ways to incorporate it into your daily routine. It can be as simple as pushing the stroller around the neighborhood, doing lunges while you vacuum, or dancing your baby to sleep—whatever works for you. Just do something.

Seven Exercises You Can Do with Your Kids

If you're in a season of life with little kids and the gym isn't a viable option, here are some ideas for ways you can be active with your kids:

- Pre-/post-meal walk: Don't overthink it—just get outside for about ten minutes at a time.
- Dancing: Turn up the music! It's good for your heart *and* your attitude!
- Sit-ups: Make a contest out of it!

- Geocaching: This is great fun and a chance to get outside with your kids.
- Swimming: I'm a little jealous of all you pool people.
- Jumping jacks: Sometimes, I confess, this is a consequence in our home.
- Running: Disguised as tag, it might even be fun.

MomStrong moms know that taking care of your body is a big deal. When we exercise, we feel better about our bodies, and our bodies feel better! Moms who exercise have more energy and are less likely to struggle with depression and anxiety. Deciding to take charge of your health is also one of the best things you can do for your kids, because they learn by your example. Remember, habits formed early on can last a lifetime!

BECOME A MORNING PERSON—I DARE YOU

I hesitate to say this, because I struggle to get up early myself, but I do believe there's sufficient evidence in the Bible to support becoming a morning person. (Don't panic—hear me out!) For one thing, it seems that Jesus was a morning person. He knew He needed time alone with His Father, and He set the example for the rest of us to follow:

> Before daybreak the next morning, Jesus got up and went out to an isolated place to pray. MARK 1:35

If the Son of God went to meet with God early, doesn't it stand to reason that we'd be wise to follow His example? In fact, all through God's Word, we read that it's wise to spend the early hours of the morning with Him. After all, the battle for our minds begins when we wake up in the morning. Before our feet hit the floor, we're engaged in a battle with the enemy of our souls. That's a good reason to spend time with God, inviting Him to guide and direct us throughout our day.

Before our feet hit the floor, we're engaged in a battle with the enemy of our souls.

Listen to my voice in the morning, LORD.
Each morning I bring my requests to you and wait
    expectantly.
PSALM 5:3

Repeat [these commands] again and again to your children. Talk about them when you are at home and when you are on the road, when you are going to bed and when you are getting up [in the *morning*].
DEUTERONOMY 6:7

The bottom line? Spending time with God is the key to our strength in every area of life. God wants us to schedule our day around Him, not the other way around. If the idea of going to bed earlier and getting up earlier makes you cringe, God understands! Remember, your struggle is not of this world! The battle for our hearts (and our time and our children) is a spiritual one:

The sinful nature wants to do evil, which is just the opposite of what the Spirit wants. And the Spirit gives us desires that are the opposite of what the sinful nature desires. These two forces are constantly fighting each other, so you are not free to carry out your good intentions.   GALATIANS 5:17

Your flesh is going to yell and scream at you. Don't listen. I challenge you to get up early and see if it doesn't become an incredible blessing to you. There are many benefits to getting up early each day, but the most powerful benefit is a spiritual one. When you hit your knees in prayer each morning, it sends the devil a signal that he's not messing with any run-of-the-mill mama; he's messing with a warrior! When you spend a few minutes with your Creator in the morning, you're inviting God to help you in your day. You're saying to the devil and all his minions, "I am on to you and your schemes! Mess with this mama, and you'll be sorry! I am a daughter of the King, and I serve Him alone! So bring it!"

God wants us to schedule our day around Him, not the other way around.

MOM**STRONG** MOM,
TAKE TIME FOR YOU—AND FOR HIM

I know you may be irritated by now. Maybe, like me, you already feel overwhelmed. You can't take on one more thing. I get it. So let's try this: don't overthink it. Don't make it harder than it needs to be. Instead, take a few simple, proactive steps with me.

1. **Go to bed around the same time every night.** Your kids need to know that Mom has to recharge her batteries too. If you have older kids at home, think about setting quiet hours. If your children are very young, consider an early bedtime for them.

2. **Get up early.** If you have a newborn or very young children at home, this is not for you. Skip this step!

3. **Exercise.** Start simple. What can you do for ten to twenty minutes a day? For most of us, this is going to require discipline. That's good! Trust me—it will pay off! Just commit to exercising for ten minutes a day, and soon you'll be on your way to becoming MomStrong!

4. **Spend time with the Lord.** You're a daughter of the King, and He wants to spend time with you. Just a few minutes each day spent reading and laying your burdens at His feet can mean the difference between being able to hear His voice for yourself and becoming dependent on others to hear it for you.

Is motherhood exhausting? Yes. But believe me, precious mom, you were born for this! You are loved. Cherished. Protected. Called. You've got this! So straighten your crown, and come up with a plan. It's time.

PRAYER POINTS FOR AN
EXHAUSTED MOM

- Pray that God will give you the strength to do the right thing even when you're weary (see Isaiah 40:31).
- Pray that God will give you the discipline to wake up early to spend time with Him (see Psalm 5:3).
- Pray that your children will make time to take care of their bodies and their souls (see 1 Corinthians 6:19-20).

Chapter 13

SEX, LIES, AND MOTHERHOOD

I still remember the graceful way my mom played the piano in a sunlit corner of our family room. At the age of seven, I saw my mother as the most beautiful woman in the world. From my earliest memories, her beauty captivated me, from her sparkling eyes to the feminine curves of her fingers. I wanted to be just like her.

As I grew into a young woman and the fault lines in my parents' marriage became more obvious, I began to notice that she didn't see herself the way I saw her. She saw herself reflected in the eyes of her husband.

One day I heard my father chastise Mom as she prepared to leave the house. I can't remember the context of the conversation, but I do remember that he made her cry. As he stood in the entryway of our house, wiping off her makeup with his handkerchief, he said, "Makeup is for *those* women."

As time passed, she carried herself a little less tall. So did I.

It was a lie, of course—this idea that makeup, or one man's opinion, could determine my mother's true worth. Nevertheless, I saw her differently after that day. Until that moment, I hadn't noticed she was wearing makeup at all. But after that incident, I noticed everyone's makeup, the way pregnant women notice other pregnant women. I wondered what "those" women did that made my mother less beautiful in the eyes of my father. Whatever it was, my mind was made up. If there was a standard, I wanted to meet it. I wanted to be beautiful too.

Children's first lessons about their bodies—everything from their appearance to what God says about human sexuality—come from their parents. And just as I was watching my parents, our children are watching us. The messages we send them early in life have a deep, long-lasting impact on how they will see themselves as adults.

We need to teach our children that their worth comes from God, and we can't do that unless we believe it too.

So where do we start? How do we pass on a godly perspective of sexuality and beauty to our kids? As in every other area of life, we start at the starting place: the Bible. We dare not trust human wisdom where these tender topics are concerned. We need to rely on the wisdom of God. In 2 Peter 1:3, the apostle reminds us that we have all that we need: "By his divine power, God has given us everything we need for living a godly life."

Everything. God didn't leave anything out of His parenting manual. By His divine power, we can understand God's standard for living a godly life. He isn't silent on the issue of appearance and human sexuality; in fact, He has a lot to say about it. Like any good father, He knows us and loves us. We need to teach our children that their worth comes from God, and we can't do that unless we believe it too.

GOD'S INSTAGRAM ACCOUNT

Culture today is obsessed with itself. The most obvious place to see this is on social media, where kids (and unfortunately their mothers, too) post frequent and often inappropriate pictures of themselves. The hashtag #selfie didn't appear on the scene until 2004, but by 2013, *Oxford Dictionaries* had named *selfie* its word of the year.[1] And I have to wonder: what message are we sending our kids in this self-focused generation?

I love a selfie as much as the next mom, but in our desire to capture the right angle (that is, the angle that hides the most flaws), we need to remember that the images we see today are temporary. I'm much more concerned that my children see themselves through God's lens than through the lens of the world. I want them to know that if God had an Instagram account, He would be following them, loving every angle and feature of His marvelous creations.

Author Jerry Bridges says, "Don't believe everything you think. You cannot be trusted to tell yourself the truth. Stay in the Word."[2] This is true of every aspect of our lives, including the way we feel when we see our reflections in the mirror. Satan

wages his battle in our minds. If we're going to do battle with
him and win, we need to know the Word of God. We need to
have the mind of Christ.

So what does God say about our worth? What does He say
about beauty? His heart toward us is made plain throughout
Scripture. Notice that Scripture describes His creation as beautiful and wonderfully made:

> I praise you because I am fearfully
>   and wonderfully made;
>   your works are wonderful,
>   I know that full well.
>
> PSALM 139:14, NIV

MomStrong moms know that they are created in the image
of God and that God doesn't create anything that is less than
wonderful. You've been created by God with a plan in mind;
you were made according to His unique specifications for the
sole purpose of bringing Him glory. When you look in the mirror, He wants you to know that "full well."

Ephesians 2:10 tells us, "We are God's masterpiece. He has
created us anew in Christ Jesus, so we can do the good things
he planned for us long ago." God's masterpiece. Imagine it! The
Creator God was thinking of beautiful you long before you
were born. In His eyes, you are a masterpiece.

Every curve.

Every wrinkle.

Every stretch mark.

That little bend in your toe.

Every part of you resulted from a creative spark in the eyes of your heavenly Father. His love for you knows no limitations; He sees you as you should see yourself. You are a masterpiece. Speak it, precious mom: "I am a masterpiece." Say it out loud. Your words carry great authority when you speak the truth.

The Creator God was thinking of beautiful you long before you were born. In His eyes, you are a masterpiece.

I know it's tempting to compare yourself to other people or worry about how they see you, but how could their opinion ever measure up to what God says? Society's perception doesn't matter—not in the eyes of God. Consider these words from Scripture:

> The LORD said to Samuel, "Don't judge by his appearance or height, for I have rejected him. The LORD doesn't see things the way you see them. People judge by outward appearance, but the LORD looks at the heart." I SAMUEL 16:7

MomStrong moms know that while the world focuses on the outside, God's gaze is focused on the inner woman. That doesn't mean we shouldn't take good care of ourselves. Scripture gives us reason to believe that God wants us to care for our bodies: "Your body is the temple of the Holy Spirit, who lives in you and was given to you by God" (1 Corinthians 6:19). But when your primary focus is on the outer person as opposed to the inner person, you aren't where God wants you to be.

And this battle isn't just about us as moms, either. Every time I think of my five beautiful daughters, I consider their struggle to find self-worth. This battle I'm in with the enemy of my soul is about them, too—because if I can't measure my worth through the Father's eyes, I know they'll struggle to do so too.

God wants us all to remember that our true worth and beauty come from being daughters of the King of kings.

FOREVER TWENTY-ONE

I'm learning a few things in my late forties. For one thing, as we get older, funny things start to happen to our bodies. One morning a few years ago, I noticed that my vision was getting fuzzy. I'd always worn glasses for distance, but this was different. Whenever I tried to see anything up close, my vision got worse. (I'm telling you! It takes the fun out of selfies when the closer you get, the fuzzier the image becomes. Then again, this may be the selfie cure for my generation!)

Anyway. I went in for a new pair of glasses, and while I was there, I learned my first lesson in aging: there is *nothing* that can be done about aging eyes. Nothing. I took a few minutes to reflect on what was now very obvious, at least to the eye doctor: I am not twenty-one anymore. (Spoiler alert: I'm not thirty anymore either.)

After shopping at Costco for some hip reading glasses, I got on with my life. But that day, I realized an unalterable truth: unless the Lord takes me home early, I'm going to get old. My body is going to age—but I want to trust God through all the seasons of life.

MomStrong moms may be beautiful and stylish, but they're not overly concerned with following trends and fads. They know God would rather see His daughters working on their inner beauty, because that kind of beauty never fades. It's eternal, and it's of great worth to the Father.

> Charm is deceptive, and beauty does not last;
>> but a woman who fears the LORD will be greatly
>> praised.
>
> PROVERBS 31:30

What's more, MomStrong moms don't worry about aging, because their focus is on pleasing the Lord. Outer beauty fades with age, but a woman who fears the Lord grows more beautiful with each passing year. In the eyes of the Lord, she is a masterpiece—at every age.

> Don't be concerned about the outward beauty of fancy
> hairstyles, expensive jewelry, or beautiful clothes. You
> should clothe yourselves instead with the beauty that
> comes from within, the unfading beauty of a gentle
> and quiet spirit, which is so precious to God.
>
> I PETER 3:3-4

When you choose to trust God and what He says about true beauty, your trust is well placed, not only for you but also for your children, because when you see yourself through God's eyes, you can teach your children to do the same.

BEYOUTIFUL MARRIAGE

Yesterday as I stepped out of the shower, I stopped for a moment and took in my reflection—something I don't do very often. I won't lie: seven children and forty-seven years have taken a toll on my body. A wave of insecurity washed over me as I noticed an older woman staring back from the mirror. I didn't like what I saw.

Stretch marks. A lot of them. My legs showed signs of aging. And my tummy. Ugh, don't get me started. Certain things aren't where they used to be. Let's just say that I'm not going to be a cover girl for *Shape* magazine anytime soon.

In the middle of my self-criticism, God's Word echoed in my heart: "He has made everything beautiful in its time" (Ecclesiastes 3:11, NIV).

In its time.

My time has come and gone, I thought.

I've had this conversation many times with my husband over the course of our twenty-eight-year marriage. I've told him how embarrassed I feel at the sight of me, and it has turned into a classic case of he said/she said. I've spoken with many women over the years about this question, and most of us have issues with our bodies. Today I'm here to tell you that I think most of us women have it wrong. You see, we may not always like what we see in the mirror, but that's not what drives a wedge between a husband and a wife when it comes to the sexual part of their relationship. It's the perception that *we don't measure up* that keeps us literally in the dark when our husbands might like the lights on! (Can you relate?) Couple that with a wrong understanding of our worth in the eyes of God, and it's a recipe for serious trouble in a marriage.

I've had the opportunity to talk with many married couples on this topic, as my husband and I often do marriage workshops together. Most men whose marriages are healthy have told us that their wives don't see themselves the way they see them. We may see dimples on our thighs or sagging breasts, but they just see thighs and breasts! It's true. Ask your husband—I dare you!

Almost every husband we've talked to says he doesn't even notice the flaws in his wife's body. He just wants his wife to want him! So why is it so hard for us to love the bodies we have? Because we've bought into the lie that beauty is limited to what we see on the covers of magazines.

Women don't have to be overweight to struggle with their self-esteem in this area either. Every woman who is trying to compete with airbrushed models on magazine covers and in online ads is a target for this kind of misguided thinking. It's a sensitive topic, isn't it? I'd venture to guess that I'm not alone in my struggle with the full-length mirror.

> *I'd venture to guess that I'm not alone in my struggle with the full-length mirror.*

But I'm learning something. This belief that we're not beautiful unless we all look like supermodels is an intimacy-robbing, joy-stealing, strength-sucking lie that began with that first lie in the Garden of Eden. Before Eve sinned, she wasn't concerned with the way her body looked. But after the Fall, the Bible records that both Adam and Eve were naked and ashamed (see Genesis 3:10). It has been that way ever since. Insecurity, it turns out, has deep roots.

Every generation has its version of the "ideal woman." Unfortunately, we live in the generation that no longer appreciates curves on women. That's a real struggle for moms like me, especially after childbearing. Why, why, *why* is our culture so obsessed with being skinny? I don't know, but we have bought into it, haven't we? Somewhere along the way, we started believing skinny is the ideal too.

I thank God for the perspective my husband brings to this tender topic, because he always brings me back to reality. After he caught me looking disapprovingly at my reflection, he said, "Since when has it been unattractive to have hips? Since when does 'attractive' only fit inside a size 6 pair of pants?" (I'm telling you, someone really ought to marry that man!)

As mothers, what we believe about our own bodies becomes a crucial part of what our kids will believe about theirs.

God's original intent was that a husband and a wife would be one flesh—without the shame and embarrassment the world has put on us. A right perspective on our bodies brings us confidence and keeps us from constantly trying to measure up to *Shape* magazine's airbrushed cover models.

Oh, and one more thing: there are several perks to loving the body God gave you, flaws and all. Women who love their bodies will tell you that they enjoy sex more with their husbands and have better relationships with others in general. Why? Because they radiate the self-confidence that comes from their Creator.

Moms, we need this truth to get deep into our hearts. As mothers, what we believe about our own bodies becomes a crucial part of what our kids will believe about theirs. We've got to get this right.

By the way, has anyone ever told you how beautiful you are?

TO MOTHERS OF SONS

No matter what you read in magazines or blogs or hear in pop culture, I'm here to say it out loud: boys and girls are different! This is good—and it's by design. Most mothers can testify to the fact that their boys will make guns out of Popsicle sticks without having someone teach them how. It's built into them— this desire to protect and provide. And it's part of God's design.

My sons are practically grown now, but nothing—and I mean *nothing*—compares to having those two tall towers wrap their protective arms around me. I'm so glad God surprised me with boys! I turn into a puddle of emotions around my young men, and I can honestly say I miss having them at home. But boys need to become men, and to do that, they need to leave the nest.

The process of raising boys to be men is not a cakewalk. I called a friend a few years ago, lamenting that my boys' one goal seemed to be to wear me down. Actually, I believe I might have used the phrase "They're trying to kill me," but

I can't be sure! If you have raised a son to adulthood, can I just give you a high five and a wink right now? Because *for the love*! The teen years in particular can be a struggle, as our young men stretch their wings and try to assert their leadership skills when they aren't needed (or appreciated!). But hang in there, mom. Stay with it. It won't be easy, but I promise you it will be worth it.

MomStrong moms know that they have a responsibility to teach their sons how to treat a woman. Now, I know many of you think that chivalry is dead. I say we resurrect it. Let's teach our sons to hold doors open for women and to let them be served first at the dinner table. And we teach them that it is never, *ever* okay to hit a woman. Our sons know that their father and I expect them to treat every woman in their lives—including me—with respect and kindness.

Trust me, when your daughters start dating, this will become extremely important to you. Watch how your daughter's young man treats his mom. You can learn a lot about a man by the way he treats his mom. And moms, your boys are learning how to treat their wives by noticing, even subconsciously, the way you allow them to treat you. A young man who raises his voice or his hand to you will do the same to his wife. Our sons need to know what God says about their roles as future husbands. God's Word is clear on this topic:

> Husbands must give honor to your wives. Treat your
> wife with understanding as you live together. She may
> be weaker than you are, but she is your equal partner in
> God's gift of new life. Treat her as you should so your
> prayers will not be hindered. I PETER 3:7

Think about this: every man you encounter today—for better or worse—was someone's little boy at one time. You've been given the chance to change our culture for the better by raising your little boys to be strong, respectful men.

Never forget that your boys are on loan to you and that your time with them is short. So be intentional about making eternal investments in the lives of your sons. Impart truth. Teach chivalry. Model beauty. Laugh. Get muddy. MomStrong moms don't buy the lie that their boys can't be men. They were *designed* to grow from boys to men, and you were given the task of preparing them for adulthood. Take the job of teaching your boys to be men as a holy calling. They'll thank you later, and so will their wives.

TO MOTHERS OF DAUGHTERS

Daughter. There's something inherently beautiful about that word. I can honestly say I've loved being a mom to five daughters. It gives me joy to watch them become young women. When our girls are little, they love every outfit we pick out for them, wear any ponytail holder, value our suggestions, and marvel at our wisdom. Then they turn thirteen. Or maybe it's twelve. Or fourteen. Somewhere in there, things get real.

Mothering daughters can be challenging, especially when they hit the hormone years. In case you somehow still have the idea that life at my home is more idyllic than life at your house, allow me to set the record straight: my home is no doubt a lot like yours. We've had our share of "epic" moments, many of them fueled by dueling mother/daughter hormones. But even though emotions can run high between moms and their daughters, lately I've been thinking about the incredible privilege it is to raise a new generation of mothers. The scope of your impact will go far beyond your four walls. When used in harmony with the Holy Spirit, your influence has the power to change the culture and make an eternal impact on the Kingdom.

A few months ago, our second daughter moved into her first "real" home. As is the tradition in our family, I went over a few weeks after she'd gotten settled in with a housewarming present: my mixer. When our daughters move out, they get to take my mixer with them. This tradition was started by my mom, and I've carried it on for my own daughters as well. The reason I love this tradition so much is that the mixer represents the memories we made together while our daughters were at home. A lifetime of laughter, recipe failures, Christmas cookies, Thanksgiving scones, and birthday cakes are represented in that one simple gift. It also says, "Now it's your turn to create new memories with your own family." (Also, I get to buy myself a new mixer. #winning)

Life seems to be moving especially quickly since the introduction of grandchildren into our family. Watching my daughters become best friends (after barely surviving the room-sharing teen years) and then go from sisters to mother/aunt overnight is proving to be one of the best reasons for surviving those epic moments that made me feel like a mothering failure.

Occasionally I have a moment to look through old photos, and do you know what I'm finding? The precious moments aren't always in the pictures. The magic—the glue, if you will—of mothering is often found in the most mundane moments. It's found in those rare moments of sharing solicited advice with a brokenhearted teenager, talking over a bubbling pot of spaghetti sauce, and wrapping a four-year-old up in a fresh-from-the-dryer blanket just before bedtime.

As I think back to the image of my mom as she played the piano, I'm reminded that my girls are watching me in much the same way that I watched her. Every time I make a pot of chicken soup, I'm being carefully observed by little eyes. And the impact I'm having on their lives will go far beyond recipes and homemaking skills. I'm teaching our girls how to see themselves by the way I carry myself and through the words I speak about myself. If they see a mom who is confident and secure in who she is, they're more likely to be confident as they grow into adulthood. If they see their mom going to the Word of God for answers, they're likely to do the same. When I look at myself through my daughters' eyes, I want to see a woman after God's own heart—not a perfect mom by any stretch, but a woman who is healthy and whole.

If our daughters see a mom who is confident and secure in who she is, they're more likely to be confident as they grow into adulthood.

I don't want my children to see a woman who is obsessed with her weight or outer beauty. Instead, I want them to see their mom as a woman who takes care of herself, inside and out. I want them to see balance.

It's a challenge for every mom to learn to see herself through her daughter's eyes. There's no doubt my children have seen me at my worst. But I believe in grace, and so should you. In the end, grace wins the day.

Also, if you have a daughter who is planning on moving out soon, it might be time to start thinking about sending your mixer with her.

MOM**STRONG** MOM,
YOU ARE GOD'S MASTERPIECE

MomStrong moms know who they are in Christ, and they radiate a beauty that shines. Remember, you were created in His image! You are His masterpiece. Don't fall prey to Satan's lies and waste your time trying to conform to the world's perception of beauty.

You are already beautiful in the eyes of God, so rather than obsessing over outer beauty, focus on cultivating inner beauty—spiritual beauty. Don't be afraid to let your light shine! Your kids are watching, and besides . . . motherhood looks good on you!

PRAYER POINTS FOR A
BEAUTIFUL MOM

- Pray that God will help you see yourself as beautiful—the way He sees you (see Psalm 139:14).
- Pray that God will help you teach your sons how women should be treated (see 1 Peter 3:7).
- Pray that God will help you model healthy femininity for your daughters (see Proverbs 31:30).

IT TAKES
A VILLAGE

I'll always remember the first time I met my friend Durenda. Jay and I had just moved six hours north from our home in a quiet community south of Portland, Oregon, to settle in another small town just north of Seattle, where Jay had undertaken a new position as worship pastor.

Being a pastor's wife can be a lonely role, and Durenda seemed to sense right away that I was going to need a friend. One Sunday shortly after our arrival, she stopped me in the entryway of the church and said, "Hi! I'm Durenda Wilson. Would you like to come over for coffee sometime?"

In that moment, Durenda was the picture of grace to me. She was holding a baby, and a couple of little ones were happily darting back and forth around her, yet she didn't seem remotely flustered. She was comfortable in her own mommy skin.

This, I thought, *is a woman I can learn from.*

I happily accepted her invitation, and we began talking about a date that might work. As we started to share a little more about our respective families, I asked Durenda how many kids she had.

"Oh, five," she replied nonchalantly.

"Excuse me?" I gasped. "Did you say *five?*" At the time, I had only three kids, and frankly, the thought of adding two more into the mix was incomprehensible to me. The sheer bravery this woman exhibited by committing to make dinner for seven human beings every. single. night. was nothing short of mind numbing to a run-of-the-mill mom like me. I couldn't even fathom giving birth five times, let alone wrangling five little ones in and out of cribs, car seats, and Costco. I'd already experienced my share of harrowing events with what was now an *obviously* insignificant number of children.

I'm sure my expression said it all, because after a few moments, Durenda felt the need to explain to me *why* she had five children. "The childbearing years go by so fast!" she said, smiling wryly.

I didn't skip a beat. "Well, you're certainly making the most of them!"

That was nearly eighteen years ago. Apparently, I got over my shock about Durenda's five children, because as you know, I ended up with *seven.* (By the way, not that we're keeping score, but Durenda went on to have three more children.) Over the course of our friendship (most of which has been long distance after my family moved), we have shared everything from the heartache of miscarriages to the joyful chaos of having multiple toddlers and newborns in our homes at once. Of course, we didn't know it then, but God was in the early stages of using this thing we call motherhood to grow and challenge us. We were only just beginning to learn what it means to lean in to Him.

That's why it's so important for moms to form strong relationships with other moms—so we can learn from each other. God's Word is clear on the importance of human influence in our lives:

> Walk with the wise and become wise.
>
> PROVERBS 13:20

> Get all the advice and instruction you can,
>   so you will be wise the rest of your life.
>
> PROVERBS 19:20

> As iron sharpens iron,
>   so a friend sharpens a friend.
>
> PROVERBS 27:17

Throughout my twenty-six years of mothering, I've noticed two things in particular that can take strong moms and make them weak. The first is not knowing we're born with a purpose (see chapter 5 for more on that). The second is isolation. Isolation can be devastating to a mom. According to Dr. Elizabeth Lombardo, a psychologist and mother of two, "Kids are great, [but] having conversations with children only over the course of the day can be isolating. Social isolation can often lead to feeling sad and resentful."[1]

Studies back up this idea. A Gallup poll found that many stay-at-home moms are prone to depression.[2] Isolation contributes to depression, anger, and sadness by feeding on our fears about our worth and purpose. That's why the devil works so hard to keep mothers feeling isolated and alone: he knows that if moms are distracted from their mission, their children are much easier targets. See if you recognize any of these isolation-inducing circumstances:

- newborns
- toddlers
- homeschooling
- homework
- sick children
- PMS
- laundry
- exhaustion

No matter what life stage we're in, there are always legitimate excuses for not reaching out and being part of a community. The reasons for isolation may change as our children age, but the net result is the same: being disconnected from the lifeline of other moms. Moms who are involved in community and fully engaged with other mothers just do better.

Some moms sacrifice what is good for them on the altar of what is good for their children. We all need to connect with other moms, so don't let this false sense of guilt keep you from reaching out beyond the four walls of your home. Most of us moms will admit, if we're honest, that as much as we love our children, the little people we pour our lives into all day cannot be our only people. Moms need other moms. Building strong friendships is foundational to becoming MomStrong.

Building strong friendships is foundational to becoming MomStrong.

Sometimes it takes a friend who knows what you're going through to cheer you up and say, "Don't quit!" when you've reached your wits' end or to say, "Give it up already!" when you need to let go but you're struggling to do so. And when words aren't enough, your friend might even stop by your house with a half gallon of ice cream and a can of whipped cream. (And sprinkles. Real friends *always* bring sprinkles.)

THE RISE AND FALL OF BRICK-AND-MORTAR FRIENDSHIPS

Do you remember when you opened your first e-mail? I do—I'm a dinosaur like that. (Hear me roar.) In August of 1996, a company called Juno started a free e-mail service, and my husband installed it on our massive desktop computer. ('Member those?)

Sometime around the midnineties, communication began its slow but steady transition from face-to-face conversations to virtual interactions: chat rooms, texting, Facebook, Instagram, Twitter. Since then, our relationships have been gradually turning from brick-and-mortar friendships into virtual ones.

And why not? Online relationships promise welcome relief from the pressures of IRL (in-real-life) relationships.

Think about it:

- Online is clean. In person is messy.
- Online is fast—say what we want and keep moving. In person? Not so much.
- Online relationships make us feel protected. Real relationships expose vulnerabilities.
- Online, we can be whoever we want. IRL, it's pretty obvious who we are.

As a blogger, I've seen up close and personal what happens when we spend more time cultivating online relationships than we do interacting with people we can see, hear, and touch. Now to be fair, I do believe in being part of an online community. Over the years, I've developed several genuine relationships with other blogging moms, and I run a thriving, active community at The Busy Mom on Facebook. But I'm here to tell you something: a person can have 250,000 followers on Facebook and still be very lonely.

A person can have 250,000 followers on Facebook and still be very lonely.

Your Facebook friends and Twitter followers aren't going to bring you a casserole after you've had a baby. They might post "Congratulations!" online, but there's no substitute for walking in relationship with moms who actually show up and do life with you as opposed to just casually commenting about it.

Moms need to understand this more than anyone else, because in the throes of raising children, it's easy to make online connections more of a priority. They seem like less work, right? But I want to encourage you to dig into real relationships. We need other people in our everyday lives—and they need us in theirs.

We're designed to be connected with other people. MomStrong moms understand the value of nurturing real-life friendships, and they prioritize them according to the Creator's wise plan.

God's priorities, even in relationships, have been laid out for us in the Bible. We were created to know and to be known—first by God, then by others. It's not surprising, then, that our Creator has a lot to say about what comes first in terms of our relationships.

- God: "You must love the LORD your God with all your heart, all your soul, and all your mind" (Matthew 22:37).
- Husband: "Wives . . . submit to your husbands" (Ephesians 5:22).
- Children: "Teach [the Lord's commands] to your children" (Deuteronomy 6:7, NCV).
- Others: "Do to others whatever you would like them to do to you" (Matthew 7:12).

Of course, we can *talk* all we want about the importance of living in community with others, but without living out these priorities, our relationships won't work the way God intends them to. You see, as much as we want to find "our people," it's even more important to establish our relationships based on the priorities God has laid out for us in His Word. Remember, precious mom, God's ways are always best. If you're putting the best of yourself into virtual friendships at the expense of your husband, your children, or your spiritual life, there *will* be a cost.

Virtual relationships, no matter how deep, are no substitute for those we have in real life. Brick-and-mortar friendships may seem like a thing of the past, but it's time for MomStrong moms to set a new trend. This is serious, moms. We need each other—*for real.*

No one on the planet can understand the struggles of motherhood the way other moms can. We need to be able to yell, "Help!" after we've burned dinner and the twelve-year-old needs stitches and the toilet has overflowed. What good is it to yell unless we know that someone actually hears us? We need to be able to cry and have another mom say, "I get it" . . . with a box of Kleenex in hand (or a mocha with extra whip) and a shoulder to lean on.

THE ILLUSION OF PERFECTION

One of the perils of the online world is that we're tempted to present only our best sides—and we only see other people's best sides too. This leads to a trap of perfectionism, where we think everyone else has it all together, so we shy away from showing them who we truly are.

Perfection is the siren song of motherhood. The local builder advertises the perfect house. Books talk about how we can have a flaw-free family. Who among us hasn't fallen victim to this mentality? We crave an ideal. We chase it. We obsess over it. We even post pictures online to make it look like we've arrived. Yet it always seems to elude us. This pursuit of perfection consumes our time and exhausts us—and Satan knows that. A mom whose energy is focused on *perception*—planning the perfect birthday party, maintaining a perfectly kept house, preparing elaborate menus and posting the results online—can easily be distracted from focusing on her children, her marriage, and the Lord.

The funny thing about perfectionism is that it doesn't benefit a single person. When I started blogging, my hope was to encourage moms. I posted recipes for growing families, talked about homeschooling, and shared pictures from family outings. Several years later, I started a Facebook page to go along with the blog. I'd love to tell you that it was my study of the Word and my time with God that helped me see that what I was doing wasn't as effective as I wanted it to be, but it wasn't. It was Facebook.

You see, I'd been posting all these great success stories for other moms to read, not to tout my own successes (although what mom doesn't want things to go right now and then?), but to encourage other moms by letting them see me get things "right" from time to time (whatever that meant).

One day I posted a new recipe for my slow cooker. I encouraged moms, "You can do this! Try it out—your kids will love it, and so will your husband!" I went on to tell readers that I was having company over that night, so it was a good thing I had dinner in the Crock-Pot by ten o'clock.

A few people liked my post. A couple of moms even wrote comments about it. But overall, the response was less than enthusiastic. *Why can't I connect better with these moms?* I thought. I was about to find out.

At about four thirty that afternoon, I noticed that my house didn't smell like chicken enchilada casserole. This was concerning since our guests were supposed to arrive at five thirty. I put down the vacuum and went over to check the progress of our dinner—and discovered that I'd forgotten to plug in my magic dinner-making appliance. Yep. I turned it on, but I never plugged it in. Can you say "pizza"?

For some reason, I thought I'd better update my Facebook page with this news. I'm not sure why I wanted to confess, but I casually posted, "Well, dinner's not happening. I forgot to plug in the Crock-Pot. Does anyone know what I can do with two cans of kidney beans, some shredded cheese, and tortilla chips? There will be twelve of us eating."

Within a few minutes, the most amazing thing had happened: almost a thousand people had liked my post! Moms all over the world were high-fiving me through the magic of the Internet, and many offered coupon sites for pizza deals. One mom even offered to call in a pizza for me! Very much by accident, I was figuring out what really encourages other moms. It's failure. No, not the kind where your life is ruined, but the kind where your dinner is ruined and you can be honest about it. If you share something like this, I promise, someone's going to be encouraged. Why? Because we don't identify with Pinterest-perfect DIY projects and perfectly posed family portraits. We identify with the mess. No one is encouraged by a mom who pretends to have it all together, because everyone knows it's not true.

Don't you feel better? I do. Because as I was writing this, one of my kids spilled nail polish all over my bathtub. #truestory

Perfection is an illusion. In the midst of motherhood's busy seasons, it's easy to lose sight of the truth that only Jesus is perfect. If you're going to become who He wants you to be, you need to embrace His perfection and let go of the idea that you can be the perfect mom. Trust me, your children don't need rooms that look like you found them on a Pinterest board. They don't need to be enrolled in every sport or go to every after-school activity. They don't need to be dressed in designer outfits every day. You don't need to have perfectly themed birthday parties or a showroom house.

If you're going to become who God wants you to be, you need to embrace His perfection and let go of the idea that you can be the perfect mom.

It's the simple things that have the most lasting impact—reading bedtime stories, baking cookies, playing Monopoly or Candy Land on a rainy afternoon surrounded by piles of laundry. You know what those piles of laundry say to that child in that moment? They say, "You're more important."

The bottom line, precious mom, is that your kids don't need you to be perfect. They need you to be present.

SISTERHOOD OF SPIES

Of all the benefits that come from real-life relationships with other moms, one of my favorites is that they allow our friends to be second, third, and even fourth mothers to our kids.

Let me explain. There comes a point in every mother's life when she begins to understand that she can't possibly be everywhere her kids are, know everyone her kids know, or hear everything her kids are hearing. That moment came for me when one of my children was about fourteen. For some reason, this child decided it would be a good idea to open a Snapchat account without telling me about it. Snapchat is strictly off limits in the St. John household, and this child knew it.

Now before you think I'm totally against social media for kids in this age range, let me assure you that I'm not. Why? Social media is a wonderful opportunity for wise parents to gain a window into the hearts of their children. It's a great way to see who they're hanging out with and what they're really thinking. But. If you can't monitor it—if you don't have full access to their account—forget it!

Parents today need the wisdom of Solomon to navigate the treacherous waters of the Internet. Predators, porn, and perversion are all right at your child's fingertips. It's a challenge to stay on top of our children's Internet use, especially when they need to use it for homework assignments. Lord, have mercy.

So how did my child manage to set up a Snapchat account without my knowledge? It wasn't a highly covert operation: I can tell you that. It was just one of those things that happens while you're putting dinner in the slow cooker or folding your three millionth load of laundry. When Jay and I heard our child had opened the account, we made it very clear that it needed to be closed. Seriously, the hairs on my mommy neck stood straight up when I heard about the pitfalls and abuses of this particular social media platform. Never mind that it was just one. more. thing. to monitor.

We were assured by said child that the account had been deleted. Unfortunately, as it turned out, my perfect, home-schooled, honest, Christian child lied to me. And said child might have gotten away with it, too, except for one thing—I know almost all of the moms of the kids my children hang out with. Virtually everything my children do, both online and in real life, gets back to me. Especially if it looks even a little out of character.

And that's exactly what happened. I found out because a friend of mine innocently brought it up one day at our co-op. Wanna know how *that* went down?

In the middle of a casual conversation, Laurie said to me, "Did you know that your child is talking with mine on Snapchat?"

"Oh," I replied smugly, "that can't be *my* child. My kids aren't allowed on Snapchat."

Laurie tensed a little. So did I.

"Well," she bravely continued, "I'm pretty sure that's who my daughter is talking to."

I was stunned. I was absolutely certain my kid would *never* do that—especially since we'd discussed it in great detail every day for a week! Every St. John who lived in Washington State and had Jay and Heidi St. John for parents *knew* that Snapchat was *not allowed*. And certainly not without permission! Why, that was tantamount to social media suicide! My kids all knew that the consequences for breaking such a rule would be swift and severe.

I sheepishly thanked Laurie and told her I'd get back to her. Then I waited for the right opportunity to talk with my child about what I'd heard. As it turned out, Laurie was right. Boy, did I feel stupid. There I was, the leader of our homeschool group, a pastor's wife, and supposedly a seasoned mother, and I had a kid who not only was openly disobeying me but also was lying about it in what can only be described as an all-out assault on my evaporating sense of parental pride!

I'll spare you the grisly details of our confrontation. (Of course, if you live within earshot of our home, you probably heard it yourself. Yes, that was me. You're welcome.) But after it was over and the appropriate consequence had been given, my child asked me how I'd found out about the account.

"I have a sisterhood of spies," I replied casually. "They're everywhere, and I've told them that I'm not afraid to hear whatever they need to say about how my children are behaving when I'm not around."

Boom. I wish I'd taken a picture of the look of terror my statement put on that kid's face. I could tell immediately that the threat of mother-spies carried the appropriate amount of weight. Content in my victory, I grinned and got back to my day, leaving my child with the sobering realization that it could have been any of more than a dozen of my friends who told me about the Snapchat account. #winning

Don't let anyone try to convince you that what your tween or teen is doing is none of your business. You're their mother—it's all your business.

A community of spies. I'm telling you—it's something all mothers need. And don't let anyone try to convince you that what your tween or teen is doing is none of your business. You're their mother—it's *all* your business.

Of course, I don't have an official spy agreement with anyone. That part was just wishful thinking. But after that conversation, I started thinking of all the scenarios that could potentially unfold in the years ahead. I knew in my heart that if Laurie hadn't mentioned this little incident to me, it might have been months before I found out about it. That's when it hit me: Laurie was *exactly* how I was going to get through the teen years with my kids! Well, maybe not Laurie alone, but friends like her.

I had learned my lesson—or one of them, at least. From that moment on, I made a point of telling my other mama friends that there was nothing too small to share with me where the behavior of my children was concerned. We have a strict "Do ask; do tell" policy, and it works.

Look, mothers can't be everywhere. But here's the thing: *someone's* mother is almost always there. There is power in living in community with other moms. I want to encourage you to get to know the mothers of the children your kids hang out with. Let them know you're looking to form a sisterhood. Keep an eye out for their kids, and I promise they'll return the favor.

"It [is] the rule of the universe," wrote C. S. Lewis to his friend Arthur Greeves, "that others can do for us what we cannot do for ourselves and one can paddle every canoe *except* one's own."[3] This is especially true when you need more than one pair of paddlers. MomStrong moms work together. If they see something, they say something. Both online and in real life, the sisterhood is strong. If you don't have a community like this, get creative. Invite the family of one of your child's friends over for lunch or dinner. Get to know them. I know that making time for friendships while balancing all our other roles is challenging, but it's worth it. The investment you make in these relationships is worth more than you can imagine.

Both online and in real life, the sisterhood of moms is strong.

So how do we do it? Well, we start by showing up.

- Do you have a solid, Bible-believing church near you? Show up.
- Is there a homeschool co-op near you? Show up.
- Is there a prayer group in your area that meets to pray on a regular basis? Show up.
- Has someone invited you to a Bible study? Show up.

Just keep showing up. Showing up says you're invested in your family and in your community. And believe me—it will pay off. It may take some time, but when you find your people, you'll know it.

THAT FRIEND

Do you have a "through thick and thin" friend? You know the one. She knows your heart. She sees past the facade to the real you.

That one. And while she's patient with you through your struggles, she'll always point you back to the truth. It never seems to hurt as much when she tells you you're wrong, because you trust her. You might have your disagreements, but they're never deal breakers. She's the one who pushes your Big Wheel to where the asphalt ends and cheers for you as your pigtails fly in the wind. She may have wanted to be the one on the Big Wheel, but she's genuinely glad to give you the push you need and watch you take the ride of your life without a hint of jealousy. She's also standing at the ready with Band-Aids and hydrogen peroxide, because you'll need them at some point. These people are worth hanging on to.

It's a gift to find a few special friends who occupy a space in your heart with the note "lifelong" on them. I have a few of these friendships, and they have become precious to me—in part, because I realize how rare they are.

Margaret and I first became friends when I was a senior in high school. I spent that summer working on staff at Trout Creek Bible Camp in Oregon. She was a few years older than I was, and she was the camp nurse while I was a lowly counselor-in-training. (That's code for glorified babysitter, but I was happy to have the job.) We didn't become close until we had our first babies in 1991. After we had our baby girls, we were inseparable. With her background in nursing, Margaret got a lot of earache and breast-feeding questions from me. I'm not sure what I did for her, except I could always make her laugh! Oh, how we laughed when we were together! Life is so much better when you have a friend to share it with, isn't it?

As time moved on, we experienced the inevitable ebb and flow of family life. We put our kids in the same preschool and met for coffee after we dropped them off. Before we knew it, we each had two kids, then three. We attended the same church and scrapbooked together on Thursday nights. We spent a lot of time talking on the phone while folding laundry and chasing toddlers. To this day, I smile thinking about the trouble we got into one fateful afternoon when her neighbor overheard one of our long phone conversations over a baby monitor . . . but that's a story for another day.

Margaret's kids are grown now. We don't attend the same church, and we don't even live in the same city. In fact, we rarely see each other. Come to think of it, I haven't talked with Margaret in about three months—I should call her. Anyway, I was thinking about Margaret the other day, wondering why, when so many other relationships have come and gone, ours has remained. We are really very different from each other. My version of sane is her version of crazy. I have seven kids; she has four. I homeschooled; she didn't.

It has taken me a while to get to the root of why a friendship like ours is so sweet, but I think I finally know. It all comes down to two things: trust and joy. Trust has kept our friendship vibrant and alive through all these years. When I had a hysterectomy, she was there when I woke from anesthesia. I know that I can trust Margaret with my deepest hurts and disappointments. She isn't going to wallow with me, but she'll listen without giving me a trite, Christianese answer for my pain. Margaret rarely comments about my online life—she's more interested in my real life. When two friends truly trust each other, the drama factor is practically eliminated.

As for joy—well, that just comes naturally to Margaret. We have laughed until our sides hurt, even long distance! If something exciting happens to me, I know Margaret is rooting for me. When I told her I was going to have my seventh baby, she laughed and celebrated with me. Even if we don't talk for months, it's okay, because we assume the best, not the worst. Friends like that are what I like to call "low maintenance." That's the kind of friend I want to be.

MOM**STRONG** MOM, LIVE IN COMMUNITY

It's simple but profound, this recipe for a lasting friendship. Real friendships, like real food, have very few ingredients. The fewer the ingredients, the higher quality the friendship. I once told my friend Margaret that if she were a food, she'd be organic. Organic friendships are the best kind because they grow on their own. No fussing. Just a little care and sunlight, and they blossom for years and years. Even better, they flourish amid piles of manure. And who are we kidding? Everyone needs friendships like that.

A quick word of caution: sometimes, just when you find your people, life throws you a curveball. Jobs come and go. Kids graduate. People move. Seasons change. Motherhood is a series of seasons, each with its own challenges, and you'll need friends for every one of them. The truth is, it's rare to find friends who stay constant throughout all seasons of motherhood. The mom who was so important to you when you had little ones may not make the transition to the next season with you. That's why grace in friendship is so important.

MomStrong moms know how to receive—and extend—grace. And they're not afraid to rat out their kids' friends when they stumble across their forbidden Snapchat accounts. Yes. A sisterhood of moms for the win!

PRAYER POINTS FOR A
MOM WHO'S IN COMMUNITY

- Pray that God will provide friendships for you that are marked by trust and joy (see Proverbs 27:17).
- Pray that you will seek perfection in Christ alone, not based on your own accomplishments (Galatians 3:3).
- Pray that God will use your sisterhood of moms to help protect and guide your children (see Proverbs 13:20).

Chapter 15

UNSHAKABLE

I never thought I'd be writing a book about becoming a strong mom. If you'd asked me thirty years ago about the possibility of becoming a mom, I would have told you that I was the least likely candidate to be entrusted with *any* child, let alone seven of them. But that's the miracle, isn't it? God can take a weak mom and make her strong.

As I look at this generation of moms, I see it happening more and more: God is doing something miraculous in our midst. He is at work right now, using the broken, the weak, the unsure, and even the desperate to raise a new generation of disciples. And it amazes me.

Think about it: God trusts us to raise *His* children. They're not really ours, after all. They're on loan to us from the

Creator. Our job is to train these precious children to hear God's still, small voice above all the other voices competing for their attention—both today and in the years to come. How do we do that? By trusting that what God says in His Word is true. By having an unshakable trust in the authority of Scripture. Our kids are asking tough questions, and the answers to those questions must not come from people; they need to come from God.

That's the miracle, isn't it? That God can take a weak mom and make her strong.

It's popular today to view the Bible as old fashioned or out of date and to pick out only the parts that make us feel good. But Christian mom, listen to me. The God-breathed, unchanging, inerrant, comprehensive, life-giving Word of God is our only source of truth! The moment we decide that we can cherry-pick which parts of the Bible are true and which parts are not, the battle is lost. Don't forget: we are at war with an enemy we can't see, let alone defeat, unless we're armed with the spiritual insight offered in the Bible.

The battle for the hearts and minds of our kids is raging all around us. It's why we need to adopt a wartime mentality—we are literally at war. Real war, real enemy. To win, we must hold everything up to the light of God's Word and engage the culture with grace and truth.

Thankfully, we have an instruction manual for this battle: the Bible. The Lord of heaven's armies inspired it, and it contains all the truth we need to train our children for the war that's raging around them. It helps them steer clear of the enemy's camp, correct wrong thinking, train in strategies of righteousness, and become equipped with the full armor of God in order to defeat Satan and emerge victorious in the end.

When I was speaking at a women's conference several years ago, a woman came up to me and said, "Jesus didn't address divisive issues." Allow me to make a correction to this thinking. When the Pharisees were testing Jesus on the topic of marriage and divorce, which was arguably the most divisive issue in the religious community at that time, He didn't shy away from the issue. He made it clear that marriage was God's idea and that it's meant for a man and a woman.

> "Haven't you read the Scriptures?" Jesus replied. "They record that from the beginning 'God made them male and female.'" MATTHEW 19:4

At almost every Christian event where I'm invited to speak, concerned parents ask me my opinion on the issue of "same-sex marriage." My answer is simple: "Have you read the Scriptures to find out what God says?" In the end, it really doesn't matter what I think; it matters what God thinks. The same is true for the other moral crises we are facing as a culture: the assault on our freedom to talk openly about our faith, the devaluing of absolute truth as a valid worldview, the attacks on the sanctity of life, and the assault on parents' rights to raise their children according to their values, without government interference.

If you know Jesus as your Lord and Savior, I challenge you to know His Word, too. God isn't silent on the issues we're facing today. Our children are looking to us to guide them into truth, and to do so, we need to know the truth and stand firm in it. Truth matters to God, so it should matter to us.

Many Christians today are struggling to fit the Bible into a culture that has flatly rejected the message of the Cross. Think about it: the way of the Cross is radical. Those who follow this path will face rejection. Dear mom, if your children walk with the Lord and follow Him, you can be assured that they will face rejection too. Our job is not only to teach them how to live in a way that pleases God, but also to prepare them for rejection and the possibility of suffering. Jesus never promised that we would walk this earth trouble-free. Instead, He promised to walk through our troubles with us.

> *Jesus never promised that we would walk this earth trouble-free. Instead, He promised to walk through our troubles with us.*

As we walk with God, we see glimpses of His grace and undeserved blessings. To help our children find those blessings, we must model what it looks like to follow Jesus in every area of our lives. To do anything less would be a disservice to the sacrificial way Jesus lived and died. To do anything less would be to cheapen God's grace. Our children need to know what God actually says, not what our culture wants Him to say. MomStrong moms understand the difference, and they point their children back to the authority of Scripture. Rather than letting the world define right and wrong, they let the Creator define the truth.

Many parents today are struggling with this charge to teach their children what God's Word says because they were raised in an environment where the work of teaching others about Jesus was left up to pastors and teachers. This needs to change—and it needs to change with this generation. We can't point our children to the truth unless we know where to find it ourselves. We do that by prayerfully studying the Word and by getting serious about our own walk with God.

If you are feeling overwhelmed by the responsibility before you, rest assured that God hasn't left you alone in this. If you have questions, you can find the answers in His Word. In Psalm 119:160, the psalmist reminds us that the Word of God is sufficient in itself: "The very essence of your words is truth; all your just regulations will stand forever." Though the culture screams that truth is relative, God wants His people to know that His truth never wavers. God's Word is the source of truth, and it will remain forever.

There is only one written source from God, and there is only one basis of truth for God's people: the Bible. That's where truth, hope, reassurance, and promise are found. In a world where right is wrong and wrong is right, I run to the Bible whenever I'm unsure what to think or do. I encourage you to do the same—it's the only truth there is.

> *In a world where right is wrong and wrong is right, we can run to the Bible whenever we're unsure what to think or do.*

GOD IS NOT SURPRISED

Years ago my husband and I heard a sermon on the precious responsibility of handling the Word of God with care. "If you torture a verse long enough," the pastor joked, "it will confess to anything." Fifteen years ago we laughed. We never imagined that we would live to see people who claim the name of Jesus twist His words and message in order to fit the agenda of progressive theology. And make no mistake: God's message of hope *is* being twisted. The message of the Cross is being misused and taken out of context in order to make it more palatable for those who want to live in a way that is contrary to it.

In an effort to soothe itching ears, some have twisted God's clear instruction on basic issues like marriage, gender, the sanctity of human life, and the inerrancy of Scripture. God's Word is being handled carelessly by men and women who have forgotten that someday they're going to have to answer to a holy God for the way they taught the Bible.

After declaring the truth of God's Word, King Solomon gave a stern warning to those who would add to it:

Every word of God proves true.
He is a shield to all who come to him for protection.

Do not add to his words,
> or he may rebuke you and expose you as a liar.

PROVERBS 30:5-6

A few hundred thousand people follow me on Facebook. I love the interactions I get to have with complete strangers using this platform, but as you might imagine, it's not without its downside. The spiritual climate online is downright cold to anyone who dares to hold fast to the authority of Scripture. And yet it's a reflection of the world we are living in. For instance, I've been accused online of being "backwards" and "uneducated" for my commitment to the authority of Scripture. Sometimes when the virtual world gets too intense, I have to close my computer and hit my own personal reset button with the Lord. I need to be reminded that at the end of the day, His is the approval I seek. He's the One I'll answer to at the end of my life. In the meantime, I'm trying to accept that rejection, even mockery, is part of my journey as a Christian.

The apostle Paul knew this would happen (well, maybe not the social media part, but at least the part about people rejecting the truth). He told Timothy that people would eventually reject the teachings of Jesus: "A time is coming when people will no longer listen to sound and wholesome teaching. They will follow their own desires and will look for teachers who will tell them whatever their itching ears want to hear" (2 Timothy 4:3).

The time Paul was talking about is here—it's now. We're living in extraordinary times. When we realize the truth of Paul's warning, there are two reactions that can drive us: one is fear, and the other is faith. The devil wants you to be afraid. He wants you to drop the sword of the Spirit and instead be bossed around by fear. Don't listen to the enemy of your soul! He's lying to you, so here's the truth: God promises that the person who walks with Him will not be defeated. The psalmist said that those who trust in the Lord will be "like trees planted along the riverbank, bearing fruit each season. Their leaves never wither, and they prosper in all they do" (Psalm 1:3).

If your knees are shaking and your pulse is quickening over the times we're living in, let me assure you that nothing takes our God by surprise. Nothing. God has seen this coming for a long time; it's all part of His plan for humankind. In John 16:33, Jesus comforts His disciples, saying, "I have told you all this so that you may have peace in me. Here on earth you will have many trials and sorrows. But take heart, because I have overcome the world."

The peace of God is given to every believer as a gift from the Holy Spirit. Our children need to see their parents demonstrating this peace. Our lives should be a living testimony that Jesus has overcome the world. He has already won!

The Bible calls Jesus "the LORD of Heaven's Armies" (Psalm 46:7). Quiet your heart for just a moment and think about that with me. I weep at the thought of my Lord coming in the clouds for His children, with all of heaven's armies at His disposal. The book of Hebrews gives us this assurance: "In just a little while, the Coming One will come and not delay" (Hebrews 10:37).

He is coming, precious mom. He is going to return for His bride. Until then, stand firm.

GOD DOES NOT CHANGE

I enjoy change. I'm always changing up the routines in our house. Every year, our family has a different chore chart, a new schedule. I like to paint rooms new colors. A quick Google image search of my name will illustrate my love for changing my hair color and style. Yet these changes are minor compared to the changes the United States has seen in the past hundred years or so. Some of that change has been good, such as the steps that have been taken toward racial equality and the granting of rights to women to vote, own property, and get a higher education. Change *can* be good—unless that change results in a departure from the truth.

Unfortunately, many churches are bending under the weight of new cultural expectations. I recently spoke at a Christian camp whose denomination is embroiled in a very real spiritual war over the authority of God's Word. Half the denomination holds to Scripture, and the other does not. Not only is this controversy splitting their church and damaging their effectiveness for the Kingdom, it will also result in judgment from God Himself when it's time to give an account for the way the message of Christ has been stewarded. We must stand firm on the authority of God's Word. We cannot waver.

As culture shifts around us, we can take comfort in knowing that God Himself doesn't change. Isaiah says, "The grass withers and the flowers fade, but the word of our God stands forever" (Isaiah 40:8). God doesn't change. Ever. I don't know about you, but I find comfort in that fact. He doesn't change the requirements for getting into heaven. He doesn't change the standard for righteousness. He doesn't change His mind about sin. He doesn't go back on His promises. His love for us is unchanging and unconditional. We can count on Him to stay the same.

I am the LORD, and I do not change.

MALACHI 3:6

God is not a man, so he does not lie.

He is not human, so he does not change his mind.

Has he ever spoken and failed to act?

Has he ever promised and not carried it through?

NUMBERS 23:19

You will never read the Bible and discover that God has changed His mind. If you hear a teacher say that a particular spiritual truth has changed, you can be sure that God has not changed His position. There are many false teachers in the world today. Test their teaching; don't be afraid to challenge it. Hold it up against the Word of God and see if it passes the test.

MomStrong moms don't look to the culture to define the truth—they trust in the unchanging authority of Scripture. They take God at His Word and look to Him as the source for answers above every other source.

GOD WILL SHOW UP

I'm going to ask you to do something that many Christians won't like: stop relying solely on your pastor or a teacher for your spiritual walk. Why? Because God never asked us to place that kind of responsibility on another person. God wants a personal (one-on-one) relationship with you. He wants you to come directly to Him with the tough questions you're facing. I'm not saying you should stop going to church or learning from other people, but it's time we took responsibility for getting into the Bible ourselves. Do you have a question about something you heard on Sunday? Open your Bible. Get in there! Search the Scriptures.

People who aren't spiritual can't receive these truths from God's Spirit. It all sounds foolish to them and they can't understand it, for only those who are spiritual can understand what the Spirit means. Those who are spiritual can evaluate all things, but they themselves cannot be evaluated by others. For,

"Who can know the LORD's thoughts?
  Who knows enough to teach him?"

But we understand these things, for we have the mind of Christ.   I CORINTHIANS 2:14-16

When Paul talks about those who aren't spiritual, he's talking about people who don't have God's Spirit. The moment you accepted Jesus as your Lord and Savior, you received the Spirit, and it's the Holy Spirit who helps you understand the things of God. You don't need a Bible college degree or an MDiv to study the Bible. You merely need a willing heart and the Holy Spirit. Come on, mom! See for yourself. His truth will come alive as you study the work and the person of Jesus.

You don't need a Bible college degree or an MDiv to study the Bible. You merely need a willing heart and the Holy Spirit.

God's heart for people is all over the Bible. Throughout the pages of Scripture, broken people find the truth that makes them whole, lost people are found, and those who are trapped in cycles of shame are set free. The Bible also answers the question, "Why are we here?" We are here to bring glory and honor to God. We're here at the Father's good pleasure. We're here *on* purpose, *for* a purpose—His purpose.

Christian mom, you have the mind of Christ! Don't be intimidated by lofty-sounding arguments against the truth. Ask God to help you understand, and have faith. The Holy Spirit will help you!

Several months ago, as I was preparing to speak at a conference in Orlando, I sensed the Lord saying, *Speak to them about a living faith. If they're going to call themselves Christians, I want their lives to bring Me glory. A faith that is real is lived out for others to see. Either I am Lord, or I am not. Be bold!*

I knew immediately what the Lord wanted me to talk about. My hands got clammy. My heart started racing. "Panic girl" started to show up as I thought of all the criticism I was likely to face if I proclaimed the truth boldly. Then I thought about my children. I knew that modeling faith in action starts at home. All my talk of authentic living would be for nothing if I couldn't model it in my personal life. As I walked out onto the stage that day, God showed up. His presence filled the room, and it wasn't because I was an awesome speaker; it was because I was a willing vessel.

No matter where your journey takes you, you can count on this: if you show up, He will too. Remember, we are Christ's ambassadors. Paul declared that if we claim the name of Jesus, we are ambassadors for Him. He also says that God is "making his appeal through us" and that we are speaking on Christ's behalf when we tell people, "Come back to God!" (2 Corinthians 5:20).

If we're going to call ourselves Christians, our lives need to bring God glory. My prayer is that God will raise up a generation of parents whose sole goal is to teach and equip their children to be strong in the Lord and model what it looks like to listen for the voice of the Lord in their everyday lives.

When we learn to live the faith we proclaim in a way that reflects the truth of God's Word and the grace of His love, we're on our way to becoming MomStrong.

THE POWER OF A PRAYING MOTHER

I don't know where this journey is going to take my children and grandchildren, but I do know one thing: I'm committed to following Jesus wherever He leads and to entrusting my family to Him. I believe that God has already gone before me in the same way He went before Abraham, Isaac, Jacob, Esther, Mary, and Paul. By the grace of God, and with the Lord by their side, I trust that my children will be a force for good in this world. They're arrows in the hands of their warrior-mother, and I have claimed them for the Kingdom of God.

We claim our children for the Lord by praying over them and believing that God will hear our prayers. The Bible teaches us that the prayers of a righteous person are powerful and effective:

The earnest prayer of a righteous person has great power and produces wonderful results. JAMES 5:16

Imagine it! The prayer of a mother, on her knees before a holy God, "has great power and produces wonderful results"!

If you're not smiling right now, then you don't yet understand the power that's available to you through prayer.

I wish I could reach across the table right now and take your hands in mine, because this is something we need to do together as mothers. We need to link arms and, through prayer and holy intention, claim that our children belong to God. We can pray over them at night when we tuck them into bed, asking the Lord to draw them to Himself. And as our children grow, we can bring them before the Lord in our quiet time with Him. We can pray for them when our mother-hearts ache and when our spirits are bruised. We can pray God's Word over them—that as they grow and serve the Lord, no weapon formed against them will stand (see Isaiah 54:17). We can claim them for the Kingdom!

God hears your prayers—do you believe it? There is power in every word that you bring before the Father. Even if your children stray, God's Word is clear: a child who is trained to hear the voice of the Lord will hear it—even when he or she is old:

> Direct your children onto the right path,
>   and when they are older, they will not leave it.
>
> PROVERBS 22:6

God is always faithful. Always.

TO THE MOM WHO FEELS LIKE GIVING UP

Life is unpredictable. As much as we may want to, we can't keep our children from experiencing the pain of rejection. We can't prevent them from experiencing failure or insulate them from the harsh realities of this world. We can't control our children; we can't keep them from making poor choices. But here's what we can do: we can pray for them. We can point them back to their Creator. We can teach them where strength is found and train them to live by God's Holy Word. We can live lives that say, *I trust You, Lord,* as we love, teach, nurture, protect, and ultimately release our children.

It's a myth that parents need to have all the answers. We don't. In fact, as I get older, I'm realizing that I know far less now than I did at the beginning of my journey. And do you know what? That's okay. Because when our questions are bigger than our answers, we find ourselves in need of a Savior.

When our questions are bigger than our answers, we find ourselves in need of a Savior.

When we arrive at our own weakness, His strength is found.

When we are culture worn, we can teach our children to search out truth from the Bible, even as we search for it ourselves.

When we are unsure of which way to go, we can approach the throne with confidence.

When we are weary, we can rest.

When we are weak, He is strong.

How can we know this? God's Word.

Jesus loves me, this I know,
For the Bible tells me so.

I remember singing this song as a child—but as a mother, it means so much more to me. The fact that *the Bible tells me so* means that I can be comforted and reassured that God sees and loves me. It's a powerful truth, and our kids need to know it.

The Bible is full of passages for the weary and brokenhearted. These verses from Isaiah serve as a reminder that although we may go through difficult seasons, we will never go through them alone:

> O Israel, the one who formed you says,
> "Do not be afraid, for I have ransomed you.
> I have called you by name; you are mine.
> When you go through deep waters,
> I will be with you.
> When you go through rivers of difficulty,
> you will not drown.
> When you walk through the fire of oppression,
> you will not be burned up;
> the flames will not consume you.
> For I am the LORD, your God,
> the Holy One of Israel, your Savior."
>
> ISAIAH 43:1-3

Like David, sometimes we want to give up because we make a mess of things. What did David do? For starters, he wrote a psalm!

> You, O LORD, are a shield around me;
> you are my glory, the one who holds my head high.
> I cried out to the LORD,

and he answered me from his holy mountain.

PSALM 3:3-4

Have you failed somewhere along the way? Admit your failure, and then move on. Don't let the enemy use your failure as a roadblock to the future God has planned for you. By admitting when we fail and asking for forgiveness, we're teaching our children what it looks like to run the race. Rather than give up, we press on toward the prize of eternity. When we persevere in the midst of trial and failure, refusing to give in to the enemy, we're saying to our children, "Follow me as I follow Christ!"

The battle for the hearts and minds of our kids is raging all around us. From the playground to the pulpit, we must hold everything up to the light of God's Word as we engage the culture with grace and truth. So stand your ground. Be the mom that refuses to retreat.

MomStrong moms don't retreat, because we know that the battle belongs to the Lord. We know that whatever happens, God's got it. When the devil whispers, "Just give up," Jesus says, "I will never fail you. I will never abandon you" (Hebrews 13:5). Don't give up. He has redeemed you; He has called you by name. His grace will see you through.

Now may the God of peace—
    who brought up from the dead our Lord Jesus,
the great Shepherd of the sheep,
    and ratified an eternal covenant with his blood—
may he equip you with all you need
    for doing his will.
May he produce in you,

through the power of Jesus Christ,
every good thing that is pleasing to him.
All glory to him forever and ever! Amen.

HEBREWS 13:20-21

MOM**STRONG** MOM,
GRAB ON TO AN UNSHAKABLE FAITH

How are you doing on your journey so far, mom? How's your body holding up after nine months of pregnancy and the sleepless nights that followed? How's your heart holding up under the criticism of an angry child? How's your faith holding up under pressure from a culture that would have you leave the tough questions up to others? Do you trust that God is big enough to take over when your job is finished?

You will face challenges along the way—there's no doubt about it. But we can take a cue from Jesus, who didn't back down when He was asked to compromise the truth. He held firm against the criticism of the religious leaders—even under threat of capital punishment. Why? Because of love. God's love for you and me is unshakable. Love is a powerful motivator.

If there's any common experience all mothers can relate to, it's the overwhelming feeling of love that washes over us from the moment we lay eyes on our children. For some of us, the journey starts with that beautiful plus sign on a pregnancy test. For others, it's that first picture of a child who is waiting overseas to come home to us—the completion of a dream planted in the heart of a mother by the Father Himself, the Creator of adoption.

The journey to becoming MomStrong is different for every mom, but the end goal is the same: to see our children walking with the Lord. So keep your eyes fixed on Him, precious mom. As you journey with Him, you will discover new strength. Be unshakable. Stand firmly on the authority of Scripture. Remain strong in the knowledge that you are loved and accepted by God, and then pass this sweet, soul-resting assurance on to your children.

You are doing it, mom! You are *becoming MomStrong*.

PRAYER POINTS FOR AN
UNSHAKABLE MOM

- Pray that God will remind you of His unchanging character when the world around you seems to be shifting rapidly (see Psalm 102:27).
- Pray that God will give you wisdom from His Word when you aren't sure what to do (see 1 Corinthians 2:14-16).
- Pray that you will become a powerful prayer warrior on behalf of your children (see James 5:16).

NO GREATER JOY

I could have no greater joy than to hear that
my children are following the truth.

3 JOHN 1:4

This verse was given to me in an oh-so-'90s frame when I was pregnant with our first child. I thought the sentiment was sweet, so I hung it on the wall near our daughter's crib. As the years passed, I started noticing newsletters with this title being circulated in Christian churches. Ministries and books even sprang up around this phrase.

That's nice, I thought. I mean, of course I wanted my kids to follow the truth. Still, to me, the phrase "no greater joy" was just another Christianese phrase. We threw it around like the word *grace* and the phrase "bless your heart." Sweet, but not significant. Poignant, but not powerful. While I appreciated them, I never fully realized the power in the words penned by the apostle John until my daughter became a mother herself.

Becoming a grandmother for the first time opened my eyes to the fact that all this mothering really is seasonal. There comes a time when you hand the baton to the next generation, and then you wait. You wait to see if all those seeds you planted in faith and watered with tears in the middle of the night are going to bear fruit. You watch to see if your tiny trees are going to take root in the firm soil of God's Word and become like the "tree planted by streams of water" the psalmist wrote about long ago (Psalm 1:3, NIV). Isn't that the hope of every Christian mom? It can be excruciating, all this waiting. But don't give up. Don't stop praying. God is still at work.

Not long ago, I got a call late one evening. It had been a long day, and I wasn't sure I wanted to answer the phone. You know the kind of day I'm talking about—two steps forward, three steps back. I was exhausted from refereeing arguments between our children. The dishes were stacking up in the sink, and I was feeling—dare I say it—angry at one of the younger children for tracking mud all over the freshly cleaned carpet in the entryway.

I glanced at my phone. Our oldest daughter's name appeared on the caller ID. I took the call.

"Hello?"

"Mom? Do you have a minute?"

For the next half hour, we talked about a new recipe she'd found for her slow cooker, an idea she had for rearranging her living room, and a rash she'd found on the baby, among other things. In the midst of talking, she was interrupted no fewer than five times by her toddler and her infant son.

"Sorry, Mom," Savannah said. "I'll be right back." I waited, unable to resist chuckling at the oh-so-familiar conversations I was hearing between my daughter and her little boy. "Noah! Go put your underwear on!"

"Noah! Don't hit your brother! Be gentle."

"Put that back, please."

I laughed. The more things change, the more they stay the same.

A few more minutes went by. "Sorry, Mom. Be right back! Noah? Put that down! What did Mommy ask you to do? *God wants you to obey.*"

All of a sudden, it hit me—*joy*, that "no greater" kind of joy. It's something we get when we've been planting and watering for a while.

As I listened to my daughter training her son in righteousness, I was filled with a joy that made the muddy carpet in my entryway seem worth cleaning (again). I was reminded that there is a divine purpose in parenting: to see the truth passed on to a new generation, a generation beyond the one we're currently shepherding.

My daughter has been trained in the truth, and now she is passing on the truth to her children. And let me tell you, precious mom, the joy that comes from knowing that your children are training *their* children in righteousness has no comparison.

That's the kind of joy that makes becoming MomStrong a journey worth taking.

ACKNOWLEDGMENTS

Of course, everyone knows that moms like me don't just sit down and write a book.

In the midst of mothering, laundry, homeschooling, and chasing my grandsons around our home, it turns out that, for me, writing takes a village.

By the grace and mercy of God, I have a village to thank.

My husband makes me look so much more put together than I really am. He has been loving me well for nearly thirty years! Jay engineers the podcast, designs the website, travels with me, tells me when a paragraph isn't great (and when it is!), and is a true gentleman in every sense of the word. I could not do this without him by my side. Jay, baby—you're still the one.

Our seven precious kids see the back of my head a lot when I'm in the middle of a big project like this. They are our greatest joys on this earth.

Savannah and Ryan, Sierra, Skylar, Spencer, Summer, Sydney, and Saylor Jane, thank you for your unfailing encouragement and prayer. Thank you for encouraging me that the message God has laid on my heart is worth writing—even if it meant pulling all-nighters and missing out on a few family movie nights. Thanks for grace and for homemade cookies and for the love notes you put in my suitcase when I travel. I love watching God's plans for your lives unfolding.

Ryan and Savannah, you know we love watching you parent our grandsons. You put the *grand* in grandparenting! Thank you!

My mom-in-love, Jerry St. John, is the glue that makes all this book writing and speaking possible. Mom, thank you for loving our family so very, very well. I adore you!

Writing about some of the harder things in my life would not have been possible without the blessing of my siblings and my mom. Aaron, Heather, Holly, Haley, Hope, and Hilary, thank you for allowing me to watch the Lord bring healing to others through telling some of our family story. I love you more than words can say.

Mom, God knows this journey has not been easy. Thank you for giving me your blessing to speak honestly about it so others can see that healing and joy are waiting on the other side of the struggle if we learn to trust and obey the Lord. And thank you for calling me on the phone that day—like grown-ups are supposed to do. I love you!

Years ago my friends Steve and Jane Lambert told me they thought I had a "spark." Their encouragement and love (and let's be honest, willingness to listen to me cry on the phone at 2 a.m.) is a huge reason this book is in print. Thank you for believing I possessed the courage and determination to write *Becoming MomStrong*, especially when I wasn't sure myself.

Every mom who writes needs a tribe of girlfriends who can cheer her on. Margaret knows I'm writing about her—and she lets me. Melissa works harder than any VA on the planet and has become one of my closest confidants along the way.

I wish I could take the time to name all the wonderful, precious moms who have encouraged me over the years as I have written on my blog and met you at conferences. Your desire to shepherd this generation of children according to the principles of the Word of God has inspired me to write *Becoming MomStrong*. Your courage and faith encourage me. Thank you for reading, for listening to my podcast, for coming out to hear me speak, and for praying with me. I treasure being a small part of what God is doing in your lives!

To Bill Jensen, the greatest literary agent who ever lived, thank you for inviting me to the dance and for believing that the message God has asked me to steward is worthy of being published. You are a blessing to me!

And to my friends at Tyndale, you are an answer to many years of prayer. Each of you has encouraged me in a profound way, from my first meeting with Ron to the "gong" I heard on my birthday over the phone. Not only are you professional, you're a true joy to work with. I meant it when I said there will never be an author as grateful as I am for the opportunity you have given me to encourage a generation of moms to trust in the unshakable truth of God's Word. I am in your debt.

NOTES

CHAPTER 1: GOOD NEWS—YOUR KIDS CAME WITH A MANUAL!
1. "'Affluenza' Teen Ethan Couch's Family Has a Long History of Legal Problems Including Reckless Driving and Assaults," *Daily News*, January 30, 2016, http://www.nydailynews.com/news/national/ethan-couch-family-history-legal -problems-article-1.2514777.
2. Caila Klass and Alexa Valiente, "'Affluenza' DUI Case: What Happened Night of the Accident That Left 4 People Dead," *ABC News*, December 31, 2015, http://abcnews.go.com/US/affluenza-dui-case-happened-night-accident -left-people/story?id=34481444.
3. Rob and Kristen Bell, interview by Oprah Winfrey, "Rob Bell Oprah Winfrey and Homosexuality," YouTube video, 2:52, from *Super Soul Sunday* televised by OWN on February 15, 2015, posted by Christian Apologetics Project, April 24, 2015, https://www.youtube.com/watch?v=nx9XaBVjFx4.

CHAPTER 3: FACING YOUR GIANTS
1. Mary Anne Radmacher, *Live Boldly: Cultivate the Qualities That Can Change Your Life* (San Francisco: Canari Press, 2008), 4.

CHAPTER 5: YOUR KIDS DON'T NEED YOU TO DO IT ALL
1. "Elisabeth Hasselbeck: Why I'm Leaving 'Fox & Friends,'" FoxNews.com, November 24, 2015, http://www.foxnews.com/entertainment/2015/11/23 /elisabeth-hasselbeck-to-step-down-as-fox-friends-co-host.html.
2. Steve Lambert (talk presented at The Busy Mom Homeschool Conference, Seattle, WA, 2006).

CHAPTER 6: WHEN YOUR PLANS GET TURNED UPSIDE DOWN
1. Nicola Menzie, "Satanic Temple's 'Unveiling' of Goat-Headed Statue Includes VIP Tickets for Photos of Guests Seated on Pagan Idol," *Christian Post*, June 30,

2015, http://www.christianpost.com/news/satanic-temples-unveiling-of
-goat-headed-statue-includes-vip-tickets-for-photos-of-guests-seated-on
-pagan-idol-141018/.

2. Jason Hanna and Steve Almasy, "Washington High School Coach Placed on
Leave for Praying on Field," CNN.com, October 30, 2015, http://www.cnn
.com/2015/10/29/us/washington-football-coach-joe-kennedy-prays/.

CHAPTER 7: DON'T GIVE UP!

1. Robert S. McGee, *The Search for Significance* (Nashville: Thomas Nelson,
2003), 6.

2. Ken Ham, "Gone in Only One Generation: Battle for Kids' Minds," *Answers*,
January 1, 2013, https://answersingenesis.org/culture/gone-in-only-one
-generation/.

CHAPTER 10: BIG GIRLS DO CRY

1. Eugene Peterson, *Christ Plays in Ten Thousand Places* (Grand Rapids, MI:
Eerdmans, 2005), 35.

2. Ibid., 59.

CHAPTER 13: SEX, LIES, AND MOTHERHOOD

1. "The Oxford Dictionaries Word of the Year 2013 Is 'Selfie,'" *Oxford Dictionaries*
(blog), November 18, 2013, http://blog.oxforddictionaries.com/2013/11/word
-of-the-year-2013-winner/.

2. Jerry Bridges and Bob Bevington, *The Great Exchange* (Wheaton, IL: Crossway,
2007).

CHAPTER 14: IT TAKES A VILLAGE

1. Brianna Valleskey, "Stay-at-Home Moms More Depressed, Angry and Sad,
Study Says," *MetroParent*, February 2, 2017, http://www.metroparent.com
/daily/parenting/parenting-issues-tips/stay-home-moms-depressed-angry
-sad-study-says/.

2. Elizabeth Mendes, Lydia Saad, and Kyley McGeeney, "Stay-at-Home Moms
Report More Depression, Sadness and Anger," Gallup, May 18, 2012, http://
www.gallup.com/poll/154685/stay-home-moms-report-depression-sadness
-anger.aspx.

3. David C. Downing, *Into the Wardrobe* (San Francisco: Jossey-Bass, 2005), 76.

ABOUT THE AUTHOR

Heidi St. John is a popular conference speaker, author, and blogger at *The Busy Mom*. Heidi speaks all over the country sharing encouraging, relevant, biblical truth with women. Heidi and her husband, Jay, are the founders and executive directors of Firmly Planted Family, an organization focused on family discipleship. The St. Johns live in Washington State, where they enjoy life with their seven children. When Heidi isn't homeschooling, babysitting her grandchildren, writing, traveling, or speaking, she can be found with her husband enjoying a cup of coffee and the view from their home in the Pacific Northwest.

BECOMING
MOM
STRONG

HeidiStJohn.com